WHAT STYLE IS IT?

A Guide to American Architecture

REVISED EDITION

JOHN C. POPPELIERS, S. ALLEN CHAMBERS, JR.

HISTORIC AMERICAN BUILDINGS SURVEY

WILEY

JOHN WILEY & SONS, INC.

This book is printed on acid-free paper. ♾

Copyright © 2003 by John Wiley & Sons, Inc. All rights reserved

Published by John Wiley & Sons, Inc., Hoboken, New Jersey

Published simultaneously in Canada

For general information on our other products and services or for technical support, please contact our Customer Care Department within the United States at 800-762-2974, outside the United States at (317) 572-3993 or fax (317) 572-4002.

Wiley also publishes its books in a variety of electronic formats. Some content that appears in print may not be available in electronic books.

Library of Congress Cataloging-in-Publication Data:

Poppeliers, John C.
  What style is it? : a guide to American architecture / by John C.
Poppeliers, S. Allen Chambers, Jr., Nancy B. Schwartz; Historic
American Buildings Survey.—Rev. ed.
      p. cm.
Includes bibliographical references and index.
  ISBN 0-471-25036-8 (pbk.)
  1. Architecture—United States. I. Title: Guide to American
architecture. II. Chambers, S. Allen. III. Schwartz, Nancy B. IV.
Historic American Buildings Survey. V. Title.
  NA705 .P6 2003
  720'.973—dc21

                        2002153124

Printed in the United States of America.
V10010116_061219

CONTENTS

Acknowledgments

On the premise that to know architecture is to appreciate it—and to want to save it—the National Trust for Historic Preservation in 1976 asked the Historic American Buildings Survey (HABS) to prepare a pictorial, nontechnical introduction to American architecture as a Bicentennial feature for its members. This four-part feature, which later became this book, *What Style Is It?*, appeared in the National Trust magazine, *Historic Preservation*, in 1976 and 1977. The Trust approached HABS because of its preeminent role as the leading documenter of American architecture since 1933. *What Style Is It?* not only became one of the most popular features in *Historic Preservation*, it has also remained one of the most popular books the Trust has ever sponsored.

The original text and illustrations for *What Style Is It?* were prepared by John C. Poppeliers, then chief of HABS, with S. Allen Chambers, Jr., and Nancy B. Schwartz, architectural historians with the HABS staff. John A. Burns and Lucy Pope Wheeler of HABS assisted in preparation of the chapters on Art Deco and the International Style. Matthew J. Mosca, a restoration architect formerly on the National Trust staff, assisted in preparing the glossary.

For this greatly expanded edition, S. Allen Chambers, Jr., provided textual additions and changes and selected additional photographs and drawings. Paul D. Dolinsky, chief of the Historic American Buildings Survey, facilitated the work, while Martin Perschler was responsible for ordering new and replacement illustrations. This edition of *What Style Is It?* was published under the direction of Amanda L. Miller, vice president and publisher, assisted by Lauren LaFrance, editorial assistant, John Wiley & Sons, Inc.

Preface

The Historic American Buildings Survey has documented more than 30,000 examples of America's historic architecture with measured drawings, photographs and/or written architectural and historical data. Founded in 1933, in part as a Depression-era, federal relief program to employ out-of-work architects, HABS exists today as the sole surviving New Deal program. HABS was established within the National Park Service, and from the outset has cooperated with the Library of Congress, where its records are held, and the American Institute of Architects (AIA), which provides professional advice and assistance. Although the methods by which records are obtained differ today from the way they were compiled in the 1930s, the mission remains the same: to create a comprehensive record of our nation's architectural achievements.

As originally conceived, HABS focused on 18th- and early 19th-century buildings, with 1860 as the cutoff date. By 1959, teams of architecture students, working during summer months under the direction of a full-time professional staff, had replaced architects in producing records, and the collection was freed of its "1860" restriction. Ten years later, in 1969, a companion program to HABS—the Historic American Engineering Record (HAER)—was established. Over subsequent years, HAER has accumulated records on over 7,000 of our nation's exemplary engineering accomplishments. As architecture and engineering often overlap, a few of the illustrations in this edition of *What Style Is It?* have been taken from the HAER collection. These are clearly identified and credited to that collection.

In addition to providing new illustrations, taken primarily from the last quarter-century of HABS recordings, and more extensive discussions of various styles, this revised and expanded edition of *What Style Is It?* contains three new chapters, on the Neoclassical, pre-Civil War Romanesque Revival, and Rustic styles. While much of the remainder of the text remains generally as originally written, new material has been inserted in existing chapters where appropriate. In several instances, notably with very early structures, recent research has dictated the assignment of different dates from those presented in earlier editions.

One of the most important features of the HABS and HAER collections is that they are accessible to the public. Housed at the Library of Congress, the collections are available for research and review during library hours. In addition, all the material may be reproduced through the library's photoduplication service. The Library of Congress has also digitized the collections, and with a few exceptions, all of the pictures in the HABS archive are now available online. More detailed information on how to use the collections, including how to access their website, can be found in the back of this book.

Obviously, style is an essential element of the study and classification of architecture, but it is by no means the only basis on which to consider a building. As HABS continues to record buildings that reflect the richness of American creativity, it also notes structural considerations, technological advances and other features that in the past have received less attention than they deserve. Also, HABS will continue to record vernacular architecture as well as the "high-style" examples that are the focus of *What Style Is It?*

HABS looks forward to continuing its long-standing mission to record America's architectural heritage. Its achievements so far have been truly impressive, and we know that HABS's influence, through its careful documentation and commitment to preservation, will remain as notable as it approaches its centennial.

S. Allen Chambers, Jr.
Washington, D.C.
August 2002

Introduction

Style is one of the most used—and abused—words in the English language, particularly when pressed into service in the study of architectural history. This book attempts to bring some order to the semantic confusion and to illustrate examples of styles that have flourished in the United States since the first colonial settlements. The following definition of architectural style from the *Oxford English Dictionary* has been used: "a definite type of architecture, distinguished by special characteristics of structure and ornament." Conceived in these terms, style is essentially visual and has no necessary relationship to the function of a building—churches, courthouses and residences may all be of the same architectural style.

Stylistic designations aid in describing architecture and in relating buildings to one another—even those of different chronological periods. But more than that, stylistic classification acknowledges that building is not just a craft. It is an art form that reflects the philosophy, intellectual currents, hopes and aspirations of its time.

Like most manifestations of social change, stylistic periods do not have sharp edges. It is tempting to subdivide them into early, middle, late, neo and proto-styles. Some guides attempt such divisions, while others divide and subdivide styles into any number of types and subtypes. Some of these volumes are listed in the bibliography. However, for anyone interested in identifying, enjoying and defending the architectural assets of a building or community, the real need is to understand the broad stylistic movements in American architecture.

To be useful, stylistic nomenclature should describe visual features. However, many long-established terms, such as "colonial" and "Victorian," refer essentially to historical and political periods and tell little about a building's appearance. The word "colonial," for instance, can be applied with equal validity to the House of Seven Gables (c. 1668) in Salem, Mass., with its rambling medieval appearance, and Mount Pleasant (1762) in Philadelphia, which illustrates the restrained adaptation of classical Renaissance forms. Both were built during the years the thirteen entities that formed the United States were British colonies—hence colonial. Obviously, a term that can be so freely applied is not useful as a stylistic designation. The term "Victorian" refers to Queen Victoria, who reigned from 1837 to 1901. During those years many different styles emerged; to label them all by the same term is meaningless. In addition, while some architectural developments were more or less parallel on both sides of the Atlantic, to call those that occurred in the United States after a British queen makes little sense. Interestingly, as will be discussed below, both terms—colonial and Victorian—seem to be enjoying more popularity at the beginning of the 21st century than ever before. Though they have become bywords in real-estate jargon, they do not have a place in serious stylistic terminology.

Other widely used architectural labels, such as "Georgian" and "Federal," which are also derived from historical periods rather than any visual features, elicit fairly specific visual images. The Wren Building (begun in 1695) in Williamsburg, Va., and Hampton Plantation (1783–90) in Towson, Md., fit the description of Georgian, even though the first predates 1714 and the second postdates 1775—the years when the Georges of England ruled the American colonies.

Many buildings defy stylistic labels. They may represent transitional periods when one style was slowly blending into another; they may exhibit the conscious combination of unrelated stylistic elements for a certain effect; or they may be the product of pure whimsy or eccentricity. Few American buildings belong as clearly to a particular style as the examples shown here, many of which represent the most costly and sophisticated designs of their period. Designers of such structures consciously adhered to the dictates of fashion, and their "high-style" structures often served as models for simpler buildings.

Some styles have enjoyed periods of revival. The people of the 19th century had a special romantic predilection for resurrecting historic styles more or—usually—less faithfully and giving them a new life. They turned to the ancient styles of Greece, Rome and Europe and to the American colonial period. To fully appreciate the influence of a style, its revivals as well as its prototypes must be considered.

Is style still important in architecture? Absolutely. Who would have thought, when *What Style Is It?* was first published more than a quarter-century ago, that ersatz Queen Anne mansions (described in real-estate parlance as "Victorian") or pseudo-Georgian palaces (advertised under the rubric "colonial") would sweep the country in yet another wave of revival? Although American technology has advanced by leaps and bounds over this same period, and although many innovations are incorporated in the fabric of new houses, appearances seem to have become ever more traditional in recent decades. Exterior shutters, though bolted down and inoperable, broken-pediment doorways and Palladian windows—especially Palladian windows—proliferate throughout the land. The author of a recent article on real estate in the *Washington Post* (Feb. 9, 2002) observed that one reason several large houses remained on the market longer than expected had to do with style: "It has to be the right architectural style, and it cannot be garish." One particular white elephant was considered unsaleable because of its "lack of style." As the agent said, "it's really hard to classify what style it is. . . . There are turrets, but then Corinthian capitals on pillars, too." If *What Style Is It?*, in addition to helping identify styles, can point to better ways to emulate them in the future, it will have served its purpose.

Early Colonial

Shelter, not architecture, was the prime consideration of the first colonists who settled America. Most early colonial buildings were of earth-fast frame construction and offered a very impermanent form of protection. Subject to rot and other decay, but at least relatively easy to build, these frame structures were replaced time and time again during the first decades of settlement. Not surprisingly, evidence of such buildings is primarily archeological, mostly in the form of post holes. The few structures that remain from early English settlements on the East Coast date from the late 17th century and exhibit marked regional variation. The term "postmedieval" is perhaps the most adequate general designation, because it acknowledges the traditional qualities of 17th-century English colonial architecture. St. Luke's Church (c. 1680), Smithfield, Va., for example, resembles an English Gothic parish church. Other early English colonial buildings in North America reflect styles that were developed during the reigns of Elizabeth I (1558–1603) and James I (1603–25) and combine medieval verticality and steep, picturesque rooflines with classical ornament and symmetry of plan and fenestration. In the ample but plain house of the English yeoman—a late 16th-century building type that was the model for most colonial residences—the predominance of medieval forms is evident; this type is characterized by a steeply pitched roof, tall, massive chimneys and small windows with leaded casements.

In New England, where hardwoods were plentiful, the massive hewn and pegged house frame was almost universal. Spaces between boards were filled with brick nogging or wattle and daub (twigs and clay). In England this construction often was left exposed, creating the effect known as half-timbering.

The House of the Seven Gables (c. 1668), Salem, Mass., reflects a tradition of building in wood that was brought to New England by Puritan colonists from eastern English counties. It is more asymmetrical than other clapboard English houses, but it shares with them the steep roofline, decorative overhang, massive central chimneys, casement windows and two-story height. (Richard Cheek)

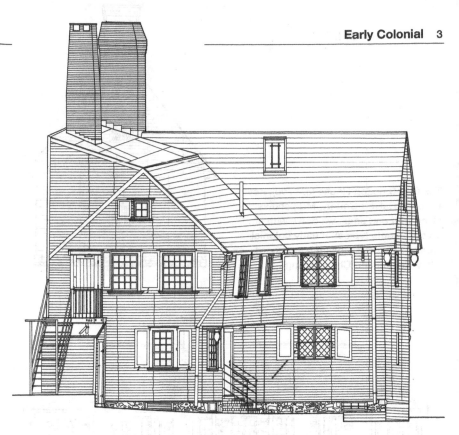

The Paul Revere House (1678–80), Boston, Mass., sole survivor of the city's 17th-century row houses, was originally one unit in a two-story gable-roofed row. Its pictur-esque appearance owes much to an early-20th-century restoration. (Laura L. Hochuli)

The Elihu Coleman House (1772), Nantucket Island, Mass., is typical of early New England houses, with its prominent central chimney, shingle covering and lean-to, or saltbox, configuration. (Cortlandt V. D. Hubbard)

The Day-Breedon House (c. 1700), near Lusby in Calvert County, Md., shows the steep roof and small windows with leaded casements typical of early colonial architecture on the eastern seaboard. (Cary Carson and Chinh Hoang)

Magnolia Mound (c. 1790), Baton Rouge, La., reflects the architectural traditions established several decades earlier by French colonists. A raised cottage, the house has a prominent gallery shaded by an extension of the hipped roof, an adaptation to the humid climate of the lower Mississippi valley. (Willie Graham and Kate Johns)

The Kautz Barn (c. 1877), near Shawnee, Pa., is a product of the area's long tradition of Germanic folk architecture. (William H. Edwards)

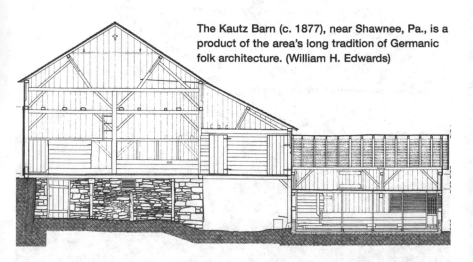

Right: The Dutch Reformed Church (c. 1700), North Tarrytown, N.Y., has a bell-shaped gambrel roof that marks it as unmistakably Dutch colonial. Washington Irving, who is buried in the churchyard, made the site famous in "The Legend of Sleepy Hollow." (Jack E. Boucher)

In New England, however, this structural wall system was always sheathed in clapboards. Second-story overhangs, central chimneys and the sloping lean-tos (usually added later) of the familiar saltbox were also common features.

In the southern colonies, one-story houses (occasionally brick, but most often frame) with end chimneys were predominant in the 17th century. An exception is the two-story Bacon's Castle (1665) in Surry County, Va., the major remaining 17th-century house with a modicum of architectural sophistication. Its decorative gables and picturesque chimneys make it as stylish as the small manor houses of the English gentry. For the most part, brick con-

St. Luke's Church (c.1680), near Smithfield, Va., is the nation's premier example of authentic Gothic architecture, with its hallmarks of the English Gothic parish church: prominent tower, steep roof, buttresses and lancet-arched windows. The date of the church is controversial. The current consensus is that it dates from the 1680s, not 1632 as had been thought earlier. (John O. Bostrup)

Bacon's Castle (1665), Surrey County, Va., is the best American example of early 17th-century English architecture. The dramatically grouped chimneystacks are direct transplants from the settlers' homeland, while the curvilinear Flemish gables show Continental influences. The original fenestration consisted of diamond-pane casements, rather than the sash windows seen in this view. (Jack E. Boucher)

Left: The Adam Thoroughgood House (c. 1680), Virginia Beach, Va., has massive T-shaped chimneys, a steep gable, two-room plan and leaded casements. While these features characterize the end of the medieval building tradition, the brick construction and casual formality hint at stylistic things to come. The house, though built on land that Adam Thoroughgood acquired in 1636, is now thought to have been built a half century later by his son or grandson. (H. J. Sheely)

Jethro Coffin House (1686), Nantucket, Mass. Shingled walls, central chimney, small casement windows and saltbox roof mark this early example of New England domestic design. As built, the house had a steeper roof with twin gables in the facade, making it appear larger than it now does. The present appearance results from several remodelings and a 20th-century restoration. (Cortlandt V. D. Hubbard)

Jethro Coffin House. The huge fireplace in the great room provided warmth, and—until a kitchen was added to the rear—was also used for cooking. A large summer beam and joists, exposed in the ceiling, support the second floor. Furnishings were typically sparse. (Cortlandt V. D. Hubbard)

Old Ship Meeting House (1681), Hingham, Mass. This drawing depicts the original condition of New England's only surviving 17th-century meeting house, before additions were made to either side in the 18th century. Unlike southern colonists, New Englanders rejected Anglican forms and developed the plain, square meetinghouse type to accommodate their services. Inside Old Ship, exposed timber-truss roof framing resembles the inverted hull of a ship—hence the name. (Edgar T. P. Walker)

struction, both in the south and in the north, was reserved for gentry houses and public buildings.

While the postmedieval style dominated American architecture during the 17th century, major stylistic changes were sweeping England. Although Inigo Jones (1573–1652) had designed earlier English buildings in the Italian Renaissance manner, the return of the Stuart monarchy from exile on the Continent and the necessity of rebuilding London after the fire of 1666 brought Renaissance styles fully to bear on English architecture. This stylistic revolution came to the American colonies at the turn of the 18th century with the popularity of Georgian architecture.

Of course, the English were not the only "colonials" who settled America's shores. Early colonial structures remain from settlements founded by other nationalities, among them French, Dutch, German and African. The Spanish, too, colonized America, and left sufficient evidence of their presence to warrant a separate chapter on buildings remaining from their settlements.

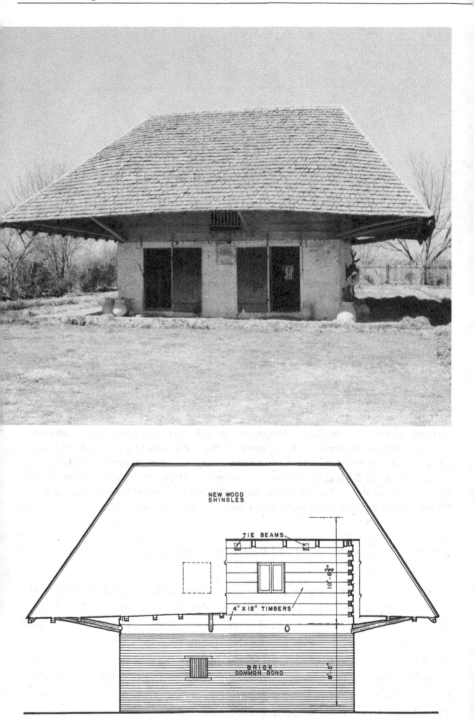

The African House (c.1820), Melrose, La., is part of Melrose Plantation, which was established and developed over many generations by free blacks. One of several buildings in the complex thought to have African design origins, this structure has an overpowering hipped roof that conceals a second story, as shown in the drawing of the north elevation. (Photograph: Lester Jones; drawing: Adolph Felder)

Columbia Plantation, Edgard, La. In this raised cottage, glazed doors opening onto the gallery provide direct access to the dining room, parlor and two bedrooms. As at Magnolia Mound, the hipped roof of the house extends to cover and protect the gallery. (Beth Benhoff, Kevin Plottner, Cheri Smith)

Brinton 1704 House (1704), Dilworthtown, Pa. This restored Quaker house displays stone construction, pent roof between first and second stories, and shed-roofed dormers—all features typical of early architecture in the middle colonies. (Ned Goode)

Georgian

Although many older standard architectural history books extend the Georgian period in American architecture until 1830 (the end of the reign of George IV), most scholars now agree that the style generally terminated in America with the Revolutionary War. It began about 1700 with construction of the Wren Building (begun in 1695) at the College of William and Mary, and, soon after, the Governor's Palace and the Capitol in Williamsburg, Va., both of which have been reconstructed. All three exhibited hallmarks of Georgian design: rigid symmetry, axial entrances, geometrical proportions, hipped roofs and sash windows.

The Vassall-Craigie-Longfellow House (1759), Cambridge, Mass., has a projecting central pavilion, emphasized by Ionic pilasters, which was a much-used feature in Georgian design. (Jack E. Boucher)

Blandfield (1769–73), Essex County, Va., is one of Virginia's most impressive Georgian manors, clearly demonstrating the Palladian five-part composition of a central block connected by hyphens to identical dependencies. (Rebecca Trumbull)

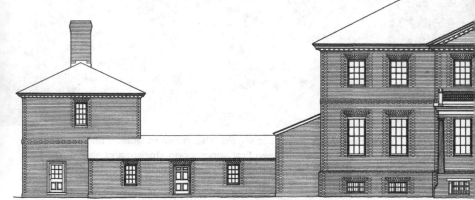

The Georgian style reflected Renaissance ideals made popular in England by Sir Christopher Wren. Renaissance influences arrived there first by way of the Netherlands and then in 1715 through Giacomo Leoni's first English publication of the works of Italian architect Andrea Palladio. The work of Wren and his followers was based on that of Italian architects of the 16th century, especially Palladio, who in turn had freely adapted Roman classical forms.

Mount Pleasant (1761), Philadelphia, Pa., has a Palladian window in the center of its façade. This High Renaissance motif occurred in Philadelphia as early as 1727 in Christ Church, but its general use in American Georgian design did not come until several decades later. (Cortlandt V. D. Hubbard)

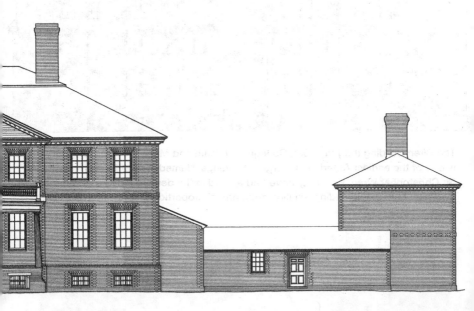

Drayton Hall (1738–42), near Charleston, S.C., has probably the first American example of a Palladian double portico. The raised basement is particularly appropriate to the climate and topography of the South Carolina Low Country. (Frances Benjamin Johnston, Library of Congress)

The Wren Building (begun 1695), College of William and Mary, Williamsburg, Va., is one of the earliest American Georgian buildings. Named for the English architect Sir Christopher Wren, who may have had a hand in the design, it has a number of Georgian features, including axiality, geometrical proportions, central pavilion and belt course.

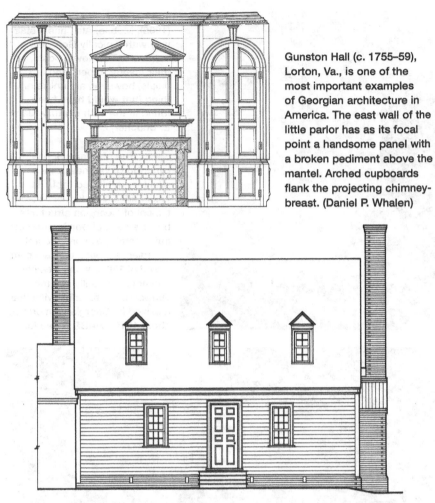

Gunston Hall (c. 1755–59), Lorton, Va., is one of the most important examples of Georgian architecture in America. The east wall of the little parlor has as its focal point a handsome panel with a broken pediment above the mantel. Arched cupboards flank the projecting chimney-breast. (Daniel P. Whalen)

Sandgates on Cat Creek (c. 1740–80), Oakville, Md., is a frame structure with brick ends laid in Flemish bond that shows typical Georgian symmetry. The breakaway chimney, in which the stack is separated from the house for fire protection, is often found in frame houses of the period. (Merry Stinson and Chinh Hoang)

Cliveden (1763–64), Philadelphia, Pa., was one of the finest Georgian country seats in the American colonies. It represents a happy compromise between the English Palladian country house and the Germanic building tradition. (C. Stanley Runyan and Allan Steenhusen)

The Schley-Rutherford House (1905), Mobile, Ala., has a stairway with typically Georgian balusters. The newel posts, with their reverse tapers and urn finials, however, are unlike anything that would have been found in the 18th century. (Jack E. Boucher)

Below: The McWane House, Lynchburg, Va., has corner pilasters, a hipped roof with balustrades and dormer windows typical of Georgian structures, but the central portico and circular porch pavilions are not Georgian, although they are composed of 18th century elements. The house actually is a mid-19th-century Italianate villa that received its Georgian remodeling about 1910. (HABS collection)

These stylistic changes gradually spread to the other side of the Atlantic. Giacomo Leoni's 1715 edition of Palladio's *Works* was followed by a host of other handbooks, all destined to influence American building arts and to increase the academic, formal quality of the Georgian style. Colen Campbell's *Vitruvius Britannicus* (1715–25), James Gibbs's *Book of Architecture* (1728), William Salmon's *Palladio Londinensis* (1734) and Robert Morris's *Select Architecture* (1757) were among them. If Westover (begun in 1730) in Charles City County, Va., incorporated only a door or a mantel from Salmon's publication, Mount Airy, Warsaw, Va., built some 30 years later in 1760–64, owes its entire facade to a plate from Gibbs.

Features of Palladian design that were prevalent in the mid-Georgian period include giant pilasters marking the corners of buildings and the double or two-story portico, first seen in America at Drayton Hall (1738–42) near Charleston, S.C. In other buildings, this central emphasis took the form of a central pavilion with pediment and pilasters, as at the Vassall-Craigie-Longfellow House (1759), Cambridge, Mass. It was also from Palladio that builders of colonial country estates, especially those in Maryland and Virginia, borrowed the idea of the five-part composition, consisting of a central block with connected dependencies. The Palladian window, a large arched central window flanked by narrower rectangular windows, was also borrowed wholesale by American builders.

The Wharton-Scott House (1906, Sanguinet and Staats), Fort Worth, Tex., is an exemplary Georgian Revival design. The giant-order portico, gambrel roof, Palladian window and quoins are a few of the identifying elements prominently displayed. (T. E. Stewart)

Westover (c. 1730), Charles City County, Va., has a frontispiece styled after Plate XXVI in Salmon's *Palladio Londinensis* that was added c. 1767. It seems uneasily attached to a facade with no other strictly ornamental features.

St. Michael's Episcopal Church (completed 1761), Charleston, S.C., is one of the high-water marks of the Georgian style in American ecclesiastical architecture. The spired tower, almost audacious in its proportions, rises 185 feet to the weathervane. (Mark W. Steel)

The hiatus of construction during the Revolutionary War essentially ended the Georgian period of architecture in America, although conservative builders continued to use the style into the 19th century. Many handsome, commodious Georgian buildings along the eastern seaboard served as homes of the founders of the nation and were sites of historic events of the American Revolution.

It is not surprising, then, that after 75 years of reviving European styles, late 19th-century American architects inspired by post-Centennial zeal began to look to their own national past for appropriate models. In their eagerness to ensure that the design heritage would be recognized, the architects often exaggerated their case. They also had to find ways to apply 18th-century details to buildings that were decidedly 19th-century in size and function, such as railroad stations and public schools. To accomplish this, elements of the Georgian style were emphasized in various ways—by change of scale, by combinations of features used in ways unknown to the 18th century or simply by repetition. It is such emphasis that helps distinguish the parent from the child and, at the turn of the 21st century, from the grandchild. Although the Georgian Revival

enjoyed its greatest vogue and most vigorous expression in the last decades of the 19th century and the first of the 20th, the "re-revival" that began with the housing boom of the 1990s has catapulted Georgian design into an almost unprecedented popularity. Huge "builder" houses, all too often occupying tiny lots, have been dubbed "McMansions," "starter castles," and "Georgians on steroids." Unfortunately, most of these, while easily recognizable as descendants of the Georgian style, show an alarming unfamiliarity with classical proportions and canons. Gables, far steeper than they need to be, each equipped with a Palladian window, fan out above cornices. Roofs are hipped and gabled several times over, while chimneys, when they appear at all, are seldom where they logically should be. One wing, devoted to transportation, can usually accommodate three automobiles. Inside, plans of such houses diverge from traditional center-hall arrangements to incorporate a multitude of variously shaped spaces. The "great room," almost invariably soaring two stories, centers the ensemble, while the stairway reaches the second floor with many turnings, or with a twisting curve. Angled walls, seldom hinted at by the exterior, divide master bathrooms into as many individual components as possible. As a Washington, D.C. real-estate agent has stated, "people want to live in a house that looks like it has been here for 100 years, . . . but they want it to fit the way they live now." (*Washington Post Magazine*, March 17, 2002). As a writer for the January 13, 2002 issue of the *Baltimore Sun* cynically observed, when technological advances "have made it possible to colonize the planets, you'll probably see a subdivision of Colonials on Mars." Or Georgians.

Bottom left and below: **Montpelier (c. 1783, 1794–96), Prince George's County, Md.** This Maryland manor displays components of both the Georgian and Federal styles. The Georgian central block, with its prominent hipped roof punctuated by a classical pediment, dates from c. 1783. The hyphens and wings, though they follow a five-part Palladian concept typical of Georgian architecture, are more Federal in spirit, with their polygonal ends. They were added in 1794–96. (Jack E. Boucher)

Left: **Montpelier.** This round-arched china cabinet in the dining room is a superb example of Georgian woodwork. Fluted pilasters flank the cupboard, which seems more like furniture than architecture. (Jack E. Boucher)

Spanish Colonial

Another major colonial style flourished in the vast area of southern North America colonized by Spain. Although a number of other European countries, notably France and the Netherlands, established colonies and left architectural legacies in North America, only Spain ranks with England in implanting far-flung and lasting architectural traditions in the United States.

The first permanent Spanish settlement was at St. Augustine, Fla., in 1565. Although some original buildings and fortifications remain there and in scattered locations along the Gulf Coast, the most important concentrations of Spanish colonial architecture are the mission complexes of the Southwest. The missions were frontier manifestations of the exuberant baroque style of the Spanish Counter-Reformation, especially as it developed in the prosperous colonial centers of Mexico. This style, which dominated North American mission architecture for 200 years, was characterized by twin bell towers, curved gables, sumptuous ornament applied to plain walls, dramatic interior lighting and elaborately carved and painted reredoses.

Frontier priests reproduced the baroque forms with whatever materials and labor were at hand. The New Mexican missions, strongly influenced by Indian building techniques, were the most primitive. These adobe structures usually had massive, unadorned, windowless walls, flat roofs with timbers supported

Acoma Pueblo (c. 1300) and its later mission church, Casa Blanca, N.M., were built on a rugged landscape typical of many Indian pueblos. (Julsing Lamsam)

San Estevan del Ray Mission Church (c.1629–42), at Acoma Pueblo, combined native materials, Indian artisan skills and Spanish baroque forms to produce a uniquely American building. (M. James Slack)

on decorative brackets and clerestory windows to illuminate carved and poly-chromed altars.

In Texas, Arizona and California, masonry construction and ornamenta-tion by Mexican or European artisans permitted more elaborate, although still provincial, expression. San Xavier del Bac (1784-97) near Tucson, Ariz., with its complex domes and vaults and ornate entrance portal, represents a high point in architectural development on the Spanish-American frontier.

The secularization of mission lands under Mexican rule in the 1830s encouraged settlement, and the adobe, wood and tile houses that were preva-lent through the mid-19th century followed Spanish Colonial tradition. All these forms later fell from general use, only to be revived in the 1890s. Particularly popular in California, Florida and the Southwest, the Spanish, Pueblo and Mission revival styles drew not only on the provincial forms of missions and haciendas but also on the rounded adobe shapes and projecting timbers of the pueblos and the grand buildings of Mediterranean Spain. The Spanish Colonial was also popular during the 1920s and 30s when Period Houses (q.v.) were in vogue in residential architecture. As before, the style was most popular in areas where Spanish settlement had occurred, and since California and Florida were heralded during these years as places to enjoy a relaxed, vacationlike lifestyle, it became associated with resort architecture. Similarly, as Hollywood became the center of the motion picture industry, the Spanish Colonial revival became the favored style for those associated with it, and for theaters across the country (Exotic Revivals, q.v.).

Acoma Pueblo has the flat roofs, projecting vigas and textured adobe of Pueblo Indian construction that appear not only in New Mexico missions but also in 20th-century revival structures. (M. James Slack)

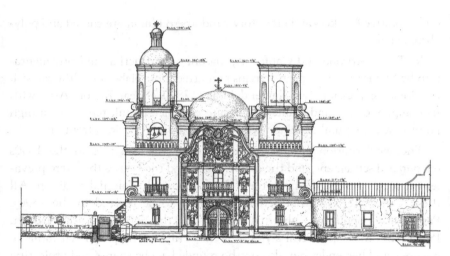

Mission San Xavier del Bac (1784–97), near Tucson, Ariz., is another of the great mission churches erected under the supervision of the Franciscans. As at San Jose *(below)*, the elaborate central entrance contrasts effectively with the relatively plain surfaces of the flanking towers. (William M. Collier, Jr. and Louis Williams)

Mission San Jose y San Miguel de Aguayo (1720–31), San Antonio, Tex., comes closer to the sophistication of Mexican and Spanish churches than any other Texas mission. The sculptured portal shows the Spanish preference for applying ornate carving to otherwise plain walls. (Fred E. Mang, Jr., National Park Service)

As with the Georgian style, the Spanish Colonial also had a remarkable resurgence at the end of the 20th century. Gated resort and retirement communities throughout Florida and the Southwest are identified by large stuccoed mansions with arched entries and tiled roofs. Some observers have begun to call the style such pseudo-palaces flaunt by the derisive term "Spanish super-colonial."

Government Street United Methodist Church (1889–90; 1907, George B. Rogers), Mobile, Ala., is a notable example of the Spanish colonial revival. As with its mission prototypes, the church displays an ornately decorated entrance portal between the relatively plain wall surfaces of the towers. (Jack E. Boucher)

Our Lady of the Wayside Church (1912, Timothy L. Pflueger), Portola Valley, Calif., is another Spanish colonial revival church. The architect used the belfry facade of Mission Dolores in nearby San Francisco as his model but added to it a doorway with Georgian motifs. (Jack E. Boucher)

La Jolla Woman's Club (1913–14, Irving J. Gill), La Jolla, Calif., subtly suggests the influence of California's mission architecture in its repeated arches and trellised pergolas. (Marvin Rand)

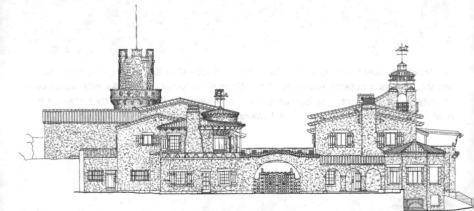

Death Valley Ranch, Death Valley National Monument, Inyo County, Calif. Better known as "Scotty's Castle," this vacation retreat was built in 1922–31 for a Chicago millionaire. The villa, eccentric in location and individualistic in design, is a prime example of the Spanish colonial revival. Red tile roofs, ironwork, gates, and stucco all contribute their part. (Jan K. Engel)

Painted Desert Inn (1924, 1937–40, Lyle E. Bennett), Petrified Forest National Park, Ariz. Originally built by a private entrepreneur, the inn was redesigned and expanded in the 1930s by the National Park Service to appear as if it had been "influenced by the dwellings of the Pueblo Indians." To this basic conception, "a softening and decorative touch of early Spanish [was] introduced by the use of adzed beams and carved corbels and brackets." Civilian Conservation Corps (CCC) workers adzed the beams, carved the brackets and, in fact, reconstructed the entire building. (Margaret A. Hess and Patrick B. Guthrie)

Gregario Garcia House (Los Portales), c. 1855, San Elizario, Tex., bears a striking resemblance to the Palace of the Governors in Santa Fe, N.M., built some 200 years earlier. The adobe and stucco house gives evidence of the longevity of traditional building styles in remote areas of the country. The inset porch facing the plaza is supported by eleven chamfered posts. (David Kaminsky)

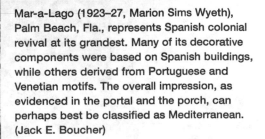

Mar-a-Lago (1923–27, Marion Sims Wyeth), Palm Beach, Fla., represents Spanish colonial revival at its grandest. Many of its decorative components were based on Spanish buildings, while others derived from Portuguese and Venetian motifs. The overall impression, as evidenced in the portal and the porch, can perhaps best be classified as Mediterranean. (Jack E. Boucher)

Federal

By 1776 a new style, created in Scotland by the Adam brothers, had contended with and overcome Georgian Palladianism in popularity. The Adamesque style was essentially a creative amalgam of Renaissance and Palladian forms, the delicacy of the French rococo and the classical architecture of Greece and Rome.

The Dodge-Shreve House (early 19th century), Salem, Mass., was built with walls unadorned except for the entrance motif and arched window. Other Federal features are the shallow hipped roof and graduated window openings. (Eric Muller)

Mantel (c. 1815–19), now installed in the S. L. Abbot House, Lynchburg, Va., is a superb example of Federal woodwork. On either side of the firebox opening triple colonnettes support the entablature. (Richard Cheek)

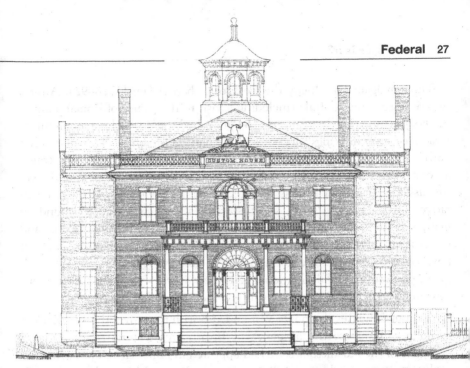

The Custom House and Public Stores (1818–19), Salem, Mass., shows the Federal style applied to a public building. It has a handsome doorway with an arched window above, but the porch, of the composite order, is more expansive than on domestic examples. (Larry D. Nichols)

Point of Honor (c. 1815), Lynchburg, Va., an extremely refined example of the Federal style, has doorways with arched fanlights centering the facade on both the first and second levels. The matched polygonal bays on either side of the recessed entrance bays reflect the Federal style's fondness for shapes other than rectangular or square. (Richard Cheek)

This amalgam was chiefly the work of Robert Adam (1728–92). After a two-year study tour of Italy (including a visit to the palace of Roman emperor Diocletian in Split), Adam in 1764 published the first volume of architectural measured drawings of domestic Roman architecture. This and other 18th-century volumes based on archeological explorations and travel accounts proved that Roman architecture was richer and more varied than Renaissance and neo-Palladian architects had acknowledged. Delicate decorative patterns of urns, swags, sheaths of wheat and garlands were found on many private villas in Pompeii and Herculaneum. The plans of houses and palaces, notably Nero's Golden House in Rome, revealed interior spaces of hexagonal, oval and circular forms. If the ancients were free and flexible with plans, proportions and decoration, then surely, it was thought, late 18th-century architects could appropriately follow their example.

Although the Revolutionary War ended British reign over the 13 colonies, it did not terminate the influence of British architectural styles. Isolated examples of the Adamesque style had appeared in America before 1776. One of the earliest examples is the dining room ceiling at Mount Vernon, which

The Andrew Ross Tenant Houses (1810–11), Washington, D.C., have simple, well-proportioned facades typical of merchant-class houses of the period. (J. Alexander)

The Jeremiah Sullivan House (1818), Madison, Ind., has a perfect Federal entrance, with a delicate iron railing, glazed fanlight and attenuated three-quarter columns framing the door and sidelights. (Jack E. Boucher)

George Washington had installed in 1775. Beautifully executed in plaster, it contains a rinceau border and festoons of husks surrounding a central rosette. It is significant that this early manifestation of the Adamesque style in America is an interior feature, for it was in their decorative interiors that the Adam brothers excelled and departed most pronouncedly from Palladian architectural design.

The Adamesque style as found in the United States is known as the Federal style, because it flowered in the early decades of the new nation. Federal-style buildings are found throughout the cities and towns of the eastern seaboard, including Charleston and Savannah, but particularly in New England seaports, where merchant princes were growing rich from their profitable trading ventures. Charles Bulfinch, Samuel McIntyre and Alexander Parris were among New England's finest of the men responsible for designing these elegant houses.

Second Harrison Gray Otis House (1800–02, Charles Bulfinch), Boston, Mass. The second of three mansions that Otis commissioned Bulfinch to design presents a rectangular brick facade with tentatively applied details. Tall windows on the ground floor are framed by shallow segmental arches suggesting an arcade. Above, a narrow stone belt course serves as a base for thin pilasters. The house has an unusual width of four bays, rather than the more normal three or five. The entrance is on a side elevation. (George M. Cushing)

The Federal-style houses they planned were generally square or rectangular, brick or frame, three stories high, and topped with low hipped roofs, often with balustrades. Door and window openings were beautifully scaled and articulated, frequently incorporating fan and oval forms. Columns and moldings were narrow, chaste and delicate compared to the robust features of the earlier Georgian style. In general, exterior decoration was confined to a porch or entrance motif. Interiors differed most noticeably from earlier styles. Rooms were not square or rectangular but oval, circular or octagonal. Mantels, cornices, door and window frames and ceilings were decorated with delicate rosettes, urns, swags, oval patera, and reeded colonnettes or pilasters. Benjamin H. Latrobe, who will be discussed in the chapter on Greek Revival, thought such decoration, especially as practiced by Philadelphia craftsmen, had gone too far. In a December 11, 1816, letter to John Wickham, he deplored mantels that were, to him, "all spindle shanked, gouty legged, jewelled, dropsical, cryspaglactic" or worse.

One of the most notable Federal buildings to the south is the Octagon (1799, William Thornton), Washington, D.C., built as the town house of Col. John Tayloe. Its polygonal floor plan and circular rooms illustrate the freedom of expression possible in Federal design. The Nathaniel Russell and William Blacklock houses in Charleston, S.C., both built in the first decade of the 19th century, are also excellent examples of the style.

The Derby Summer House (1794, Samuel McIntyre), Danvers, Mass., is an elegant example of the Federal style. The festoons above the rectangular second-story windows and the urns are typical Federal decorations. Built in Peabody, Mass., the pavilion was moved to Danvers in 1904. (Cervin Robinson)

Halcyon House (1787), Washington, D.C. The restored south front of this Georgetown mansion is a masterpiece of the Federal style. To either side of the arched doorway, framed with pilasters supporting a pediment, first-floor windows have sashes with nine panes each (nine-over nine). Second-floor windows, properly scaled, have nine-over-six, while third-floor dormers have six-over-six. (Jack E. Boucher)

Neoclassical

In 1784, while serving as United States minister to France, Thomas Jefferson received a request for assistance in designing a new capitol for his native state, Virginia. In turn Jefferson obtained assistance from French architect Charles-Louis Clérisseau. They used as their model the Maison Carrée, an ancient Roman temple in Nîmes. The capitol was an immediate success, and its influence was enormous. The first use of the antique temple form in a public building, it set the style for civic structures across the country, and—although based on a Roman temple—helped inaugurate the Greek Revival a few decades later.

While the Federal style served well for dwellings, the Neoclassical was used primarily for public buildings—not only civic structures, but also banks, town halls and churches. For those wealthy enough, or avant-garde enough, however, the style worked for houses as well.

The First Bank of the United States (1795–97, Samuel Blodgett), in Philadelphia, helped secure the style as appropriate for banks, with its obvious connotations of strength, security and tradition. Like Jefferson before him,

Tudor Place (1805–16, William Thornton), Washington, D.C. Standing tall and proud on the heights of Georgetown, this neoclassical mansion was home to the Peter family for six generations. The south facade is dominated by a circular, domed portico, known as the temple. One half of the circle projects beyond the walls of the south facade; the other is recessed into them. (Jack E. Boucher)

Virginia State Capitol (1785–98, Thomas Jefferson, with Charles-Louis Clérisseau), Richmond, Va. The Virginia State Capitol was modeled on the Maison Carrée, in Nîmes, but its architects substituted the simpler Ionic order for the original, more difficult Corinthian. This 1831 engraving shows the building still lacking the front stairway to the portico, which Jefferson had intended, and which was finally installed early in the 20th century.

The White House (1792, James Hoban), Washington, D.C. An architectural symbol of the presidency, and—by extension—American democracy, the home of the nation's president was grand beyond the scale of any American house of its time. It was built of stone, rather than of the more typical frame or brick generally used in residential work. (Jack E. Boucher)

Blodgett turned to a European structure for inspiration: the Exchange in Dublin. The bank has a facade dominated by a monumental Corinthian portico, with paired columns at the corners helping support the pediment. Behind, pilasters separate bays, while the facade, though not the other walls of the brick structure, is faced with marble.

One of the most public of the public buildings of the new republic was the White House (1792–1800) in Washington, D.C. Designed by James Hoban, it, too, was modeled on an Irish building: Leinster House in Dublin. Its dignified Palladian proportions and details have served it well throughout all the stylistic changes that American architecture has undergone since it first began

Rich embellishments, such as these around the central doorway of the north facade of the White House, were added at the suggestion of George Washington. (Jack E. Boucher)

The White House, Blue Room. During the 1960s, First Lady Jacqueline Kennedy redecorated the ceremonial rooms. Choice American furnishings of the period stand against unadorned walls plastered above a simple chair rail. (Jack E. Boucher)

to serve the nation. Another public building of note is B. H. Latrobe's Roman Catholic Cathedral (1806) in Baltimore. Built of granite, the cruciform church, now a minor basilica, has a shallow dome over the crossing, and shows Latrobe's mastery in handling spatial relationships.

Neoclassical buildings are much heavier than Federal style buildings in general effect and in detailing. They are almost always of masonry construction, seldom of wood. While entries may be capped with semicircular elliptical arches, monumental porticos with pediments, which are frequently embellished with carving, often shelter them. Most commonly, classical orders are Roman, not Greek, in inspiration. Many of the nation's leaders, chief among them Thomas Jefferson, thought that the Roman republic could serve as a model for the United States, not only in law and order, but in architecture as well. Later, the same thoughts were applied to Greece and Grecian architecture.

Peale Museum (1814–16, Robert Cary Long, Sr.), Baltimore, Md. This stylistic hybrid was designed to house artist Rembrandt Peale's Baltimore Museum. Chaste brick walls and proper diminution of fenestration are Federal characteristics, while the frontispiece, with columns, arches and sculpture, is Neoclassical. The original use of the house also reflected a dual personality. The first purpose-built museum in the country, it also served as the Peale family home. (James W. Rosenthal)

Among the privileged few, some Americans sought to build their own houses in the Neoclassical style, rather than in the prevailing, and simpler, Federal mode. With an inheritance from George Washington, Thomas and Martha Custis Peter (Washington was her step-grandfather) purchased an unfinished house on the heights above Georgetown, D.C., in 1805. Employing William Thornton, a friend and amateur architect who had won the 1790s design competition for the United States capitol, the Peter family built Tudor Place several years later. The five-part mansion nicely combines the Federal style in its austere north facade with the Neoclassical in its elaborate south facade.

Jeffersonian

As noted in the section on the Neoclassical style, Thomas Jefferson, aided by Charles-Louis Clérisseau, provided the design for the Virginia State Capitol. In addition to that building, Jefferson is remembered for his unique architectural achievements at Monticello, Poplar Forest and the University of Virginia in Charlottesville. His university design combined 10 different pavilions, each containing a lecture room and housing for a member of the faculty. Jefferson designed the pavilions, each to be patterned after a specific Roman or Palladian temple, as models "of taste and good architecture" and to "serve as specimens for the architectural lecturer."

Jefferson's pavilion designs—in contrast to the Federal style—were derived from public structures and not from the houses and villas of Roman nobility. Consequently, they have heavy modillions, full-scale cornices and a more masculine feeling than Federal-style mansions. There was more to the university than 10 pavilions, however. With them, the numerous student rooms, dining hall, and the library, or Rotunda (a half-scale, red brick rendition of the Pantheon in Rome), the university was the largest building operation in the

Belle Grove (c. 1795), Middletown, Va., resembles other houses influenced by Jefferson that were often one story on a raised basement with a small Roman portico. In this instance, Jefferson himself gave "the favor of [his] advice on the plan." The formal symmetry of the facade is compromised by a side wing, which was added sometime between 1815 and 1820. (Rebecca Rogers; Jack E. Boucher)

country from 1817 to 1826. Once their work was completed, Jefferson's builders went on to erect courthouses, hotels, churches and houses throughout Virginia and states where Virginians settled. Characterized by red brick walls, columned porticoes, white trim and green shutters, they form an easily identified legacy. They could be called Neoclassical, or Roman Revival, but it is perhaps more fitting to call them Jeffersonian. Until the name of architect Henry Hobson Richardson was unalterably wedded to the Romanesque in the late 19th century, no architectural style was so closely identified with one American.

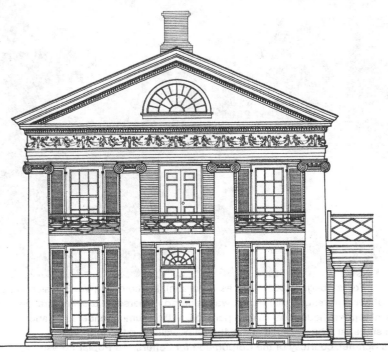

Pavilion II, University of Virginia (1822, Thomas Jefferson), Charlottesville, Va., was adapted from the ancient Roman temple of Fortuna Virilis, familiar to Jefferson from the drawings of Palladio. The red-brick walls and louvered shutters, however, are pure Virginia. (Michael D. Sullivan)

The Main Hotel Building (1830s), Old Sweet Springs, W. Va., has unfluted columns, red-brick walls and white trim, all reminiscent of Jefferson's University of Virginia. It was built, and in all likelihood designed as well, by William B. Phillips, whom Jefferson once credited with having done the best brickwork at the University.

Poplar Forest (begun 1805, Thomas Jefferson), Bedford Co., Va. Envisioned as a private villa retreat, Poplar Forest was Jefferson's personal architectural statement. The octagonal house has Tuscan porticos, with columns rendered to appear like stone, and balustrades above the brick walls and the roof deck. (Les Schofer, courtesy of the Corporation for Jefferson's Poplar Forest)

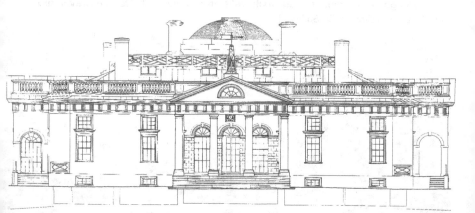

Monticello (1768–1809, Thomas Jefferson), Albemarle Co., Va. As personal a house as exists anywhere, Monticello (as its dates suggest) represents Jefferson's life-long infatuation with architecture. The house grew with the man, first reflecting his study of Palladian forms, then, after he returned from Europe, his fondness for ancient Roman and contemporary French architecture. This view shows the east, or entrance, front. (Isabel C. Yang, Timothy A. Buehner, Hugh D. Hughes, Sandra M. Moore, Jonathon C. Spodek, Bryan S. Falvey, David R. Schlensker, Andrew G. Stone)

Greek Revival

Although Jefferson favored the Roman mode, one of his younger contemporaries was sufficiently sure of himself to declare without reservation that his "principles of good taste . . . [were] rigid in Grecian Architecture." Benjamin Henry Latrobe (1764–1820), an architect and engineer who was responsible for some of America's most notable structures, was born in England and educated on the Continent. He emigrated to the United States in 1796 and by 1798 had designed the Bank of Pennsylvania in Philadelphia, the first American building to incorporate a classical Greek order, the Ionic.

The Governor's Mansion (1853–55, Abner Cook), Austin, Tex., is a graceful Greek Revival structure that has a six-column Ionic portico sheltering a second-floor balcony, as well as a full entablature concealing a low-hipped roof. (Jack E. Boucher)

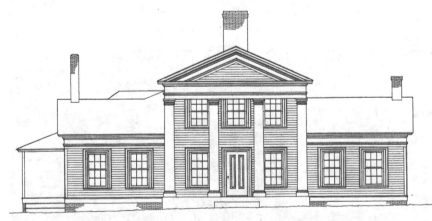

The Brown Augustine House (c. 1834), near New Carlisle, Ind., is a classic Greek Revival example as interpreted in the old Northwest Territory. Flanking the temple front, with its pedimented portico, are one-story wings. (E. J. Wieczorek)

Andalusia (c. 1797, 1834, Thomas U. Walter), near Philadelphia, Pa., is one of the most noted Greek Revival houses in America. To an existing earlier house, Walter made additions for owner Nicholas Biddle and crowned his work with this impressive Doric portico. (Jack E. Boucher)

Below: Engine Company No. 3 (1853), Sacramento, Calif., has a flat roof behind its imposing Greek Revival pediment, belying the temple design suggested by the facade. (Glen Fishback)

The Costigan House (1850–52, Francis Costigan), Madison, Ind., shows the architect-owner's mastery of Greek form and proportion, particularly in the relation of the porch entablature to the main one. (Jack E. Boucher)

The Old Patent Office (1836–67, William P. Elliott and Robert Mills), Washington, D.C., has a south portico copied directly from the Parthenon. The building has been adapted to museum use. (Jack E. Boucher)

It took a while to catch on, but during the 1830s and 1840s, essentially the second quarter of the 19th century, the Greek Revival flourished in the United States as nowhere else. These were the years in which the still-young nation was expanding at an unprecedented pace, both in population and geographically, and was also asserting itself on the international scene. One reason for the appeal of the Greek Revival at this time and in this place was the often-expressed sentiment that America, with its democratic ideals, was the spiritual successor of ancient Greece. The fuels of this patriotic flame were

The Brues House (c.1853), Wheeling, W. Va., has a Greek Revival portico that provides a miniature temple front to the house. Not content with this embellishment alone, the builder also framed the dormer windows with pilasters and pediments. (Jack E. Boucher)

The William F. Kuehneman House, Racine Wis., is in the popular temple form, which replaced the log cabin as a common Midwestern house type in the 1840s and 1850s. Greek Revival features include fluted Doric columns, flat corner pilasters, a wide, plain frieze and a horizontal transom over the door. (Cervin Robinson)

fueled by the Greek revolt against the Ottoman Empire during the 1820s. The thought that the United States could, and should, inherit the beauty and grandeur of ancient Greece was evident not only in architecture but also in the very names of newly established towns such as Athens, Sparta and Ithaca, located from Georgia to Maine and throughout the Midwest. In 1842 architect Alexander Jackson Davis complained that the Greek Revival was used for so many buildings that it was difficult for strangers in American towns "to distinguish between a church, a bank and a hall of justice." He might have included houses as well, for temple fronts were used by many wealthy doctors and lawyers to embellish both their dwellings and their standing in local soci-

Evergreen Plantation, St. John the Baptist Parish, La. In 1832, this late-18th-century house was remodeled and enlarged, resulting in an elegant mélange of several styles. The basic form recalls a colonial Louisiana raised cottage, the generous fanlights over the doorways are Federal, while the columns and pediment reflect the emerging Greek Revival style. Specifications for the 1832 work called for the stairs to "wind gracefully down with the proper slope," and directed that their bases be as close together "as will consistently agree with grace and elegance." (Nancy Kaiser and Brian Polinsky)

Natchez, in Mississippi, is one of the epicenters of the Greek Revival style in America. Among the fine mansions erected by wealthy planters is Melrose, ca. 1845, designed by Jacob Byers of Hagerstown, Md. A monumental tetra-style portico, with full entablature and pediment, centers the facade, and contrasts with brick walls to either side. (Jack E. Boucher)

ety. Temple fronts were particularly loved by southern planters. White columns come immediately to mind when one thinks of antebellum plantations, not to mention *Gone With the Wind*.

The most easily identified features of a Greek-inspired building are columns and pilasters, although not every Greek Revival structure has them. Other hallmarks of the style are bold, simple moldings on both the exterior and the interior, pedimented gables, heavy cornices with unadorned friezes and horizontal transoms above entrances. Ancient Greek structures did not use arches; consequently, with the rise of the Greek Revival the arched entrances and fan windows so common in the Federal and Jeffersonian styles were abandoned. Most Greek Revival frame houses were painted white because it was not then known that the white marble of ancient Greek buildings had often been polychromed. In addition to free-standing buildings, the style was also used in urban domestic architecture. Row houses, beginning to proliferate in growing cities, came to be characterized by austere facades softened by Greek details around windows and doors, with the latter often protected by a columned entry porch.

Davis's complaint about the ubiquitousness of the Greek Revival was, if anything, hypocritical. He had done as much as anyone to popularize the style throughout the nation. His association with Ithiel Town was the first

Enormous windows and doors, all framed with textbook Greek Revival trim, embellish the dining room at Melrose. They and the punkah, a six-foot mahogany "fan" operated by a servant, aided air circulation in the humid Mississippi climate. (Jack E. Boucher)

significant architectural partnership in the country. Together they not only designed buildings to serve the functions Davis listed, they also provided designs for two of the finest state capitols of the period: Indiana (1831–35) and North Carolina (1833–40), both exemplary, even inspired, Greek Revival buildings. Only the latter remains.

The Greek Revival inspired the nation's first great professional architects. In addition to Latrobe and Town and Davis, William Strickland, Asher Benjamin, Thomas U. Walter and Robert Mills were among those who designed in the style. The style was also fostered by books on architecture, as earlier architectural developments in America had been. In fact, Davis had written in his day book: "1828 March 15 First study of Stuart's Athens, from which I date professional practice." He was referring to an English publication, Stuart and Revett's *The Antiquities of Athens*. Handbooks by Asher Benjamin, Minard Lafever and John Haviland gave carpenters across the land access to Greek Revival features, and helped the style become, for a time, something of an American vernacular.

Founder's Hall, Girard College (1833–42, Thomas U. Walter), Philadelphia, Pa., is one of the nation's finest Greek Revival structures. Unlike many buildings based on ancient temple prototypes, the marble building is fully peripteral: the Corinthian peristyle (or colonnade) extends around all four sides, not just the front. Although this school for orphans was cloaked in Greek Revival garb, the founder, Stephen Girard, discouraged the study of Greek or Latin, arguing that students would be better served with courses in "practical education." (Joe Elliott)

Gothic Revival

In the late 18th and early 19th centuries, styles in literature, art and architecture rapidly changed in both Europe and the United States. One of the more pervasive currents was the romantic movement, which proclaimed the superiority of the Christian medieval past. With almost religious fervor romantics extolled the symbolic virtues of Gothic architecture and fostered its revival.

Right: **The Unitarian Church (1817, 1852–54, Francis D. Lee), Charleston, S.C.** In an attempt to be architecturally up-to-date, Charleston's Unitarians had their church "gothicized" in the 1850s. The fan vaulting, executed in plaster on lathes rather than in stone, imitates late English Gothic examples. (Charles H. Bayless)

Left: **The Chapel of the Centurion at Fort Monroe, Hampton, Va.,** is derived from pattern-book plans published by Richard Upjohn. Built in 1857–58, the chapel is sheathed in board-and-batten, now painted white, but originally colored red and green. Simple lancet windows add to the Gothic character. (Jack E. Boucher)

Right: **The Church of St. James the Less (1846–48), Philadelphia, Pa.,** was a seminal building in spreading the Gothic Revival gospel across the United States. The first American example of a pure English parish church, it was modeled on St. Michael's, Longstanton, in Cambridgeshire, built c. 1230. The English Ecclesiastical Society, who supervised construction of St. James, had been organized to revive medieval church ritual and design. The society's insistence on proper liturgical arrangements and honesty of materials propelled St. James to the front rank of American Gothic Revival design. (Jack E. Boucher)

Left: **Organ, Church of the Holy Cross (1850–52, Edward C. Jones) Stateburg, S.C.** This Gothic Revival case is typical of the work of New York organ builder Henry Erben. Arches, crockets and finials reflect motifs seen in this important Gothic Revival church, and demonstrate the care that 19th-century designers took to ensure that all components, including furnishings, would accord with the chosen architectural style. (Caroline Guay, Michael Lafond, Timothy Buehner)

Right: **Lace House (1863), Black Hawk, Colo.** This Gothic Revival house, located in a gold mining community, was built as a wedding present. The house has a porch with delicate filigree work and decorative bargeboards in the gables, all done in lacy, Gothic motifs. (Gabrielle Witkin)

The First Baptist Church (1884–86, John R. Thomas), Lynchburg, Va., is an authoritative statement of the High Victorian Gothic style. The rose window centering the gabled facade is one of three lighting the sanctuary. (Richard Cheek)

Gothic Revival architecture came to America from England; however, it never achieved widespread popularity here, perhaps because of its strong association with Britain, liturgical Christianity and aristocracy—all suspect to the New World "democrat." The first American residence to employ Gothic details was Sedgeley (1799, Benjamin H. Latrobe), a country house outside Philadelphia. In the first quarter of the 19th century, other major architects also experimented with the Gothic Revival style, usually in the design of country mansions and churches, occasionally in public buildings and prisons.

By the 1830s a growing taste for the romantic, fostered largely by the novels of Sir Walter Scott and dissatisfaction with the restraints of classical architecture, turned the Gothic Revival into a popular movement. Alexander Jackson Davis became the country's most prolific Gothic Revival architect. His plans for houses and cottages were widely distributed in the popular books of Andrew Jackson Downing, pioneer landscape architect and arbiter of mid-century taste. The picturesque country cottages advocated by Davis and Downing dotted the countryside in the 1840s and 1850s and continued to be built in some areas long after the Civil War.

Gothic Revival was distinguished by the pointed arch, which could be combined ingeniously with towers, crenellation, steep gabled roofs, lacy bargeboards, verandas, clustered columns, foliated ornaments, bay and oriel

Cottage #87, South Seaville Methodist Camp Meeting Grounds, South Seaville, N.J. This summer religious campground was established in 1863–64, and small cottages were soon built around the central preaching area, or tabernacle. Builders of this cottage eschewed the simpler Italianate mode favored by their neighbors to construct a miniature board-and-batten Gothic Revival fantasy. Perhaps they felt the Gothic had a more religious connotation than other styles. (David Ames)

The William J. Rotch House (1846, A. J. Davis and William R. Emerson), New Bedford, Mass., is one of the Gothic villas designed by Davis that was illustrated in the works of A. J. Downing, where it was entitled "A Cottage-Villa in the Rural Gothic Style." (Ned Goode)

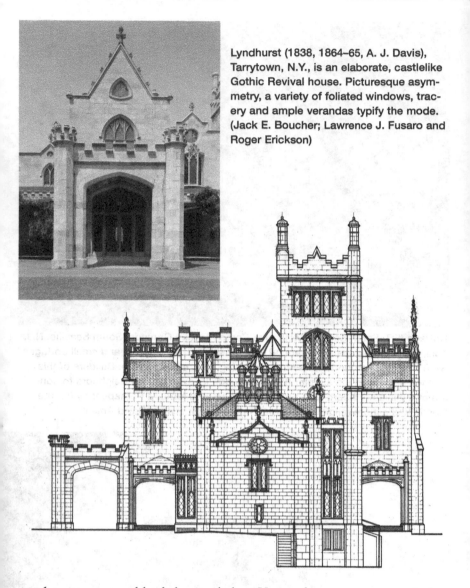

Lyndhurst (1838, 1864–65, A. J. Davis), Tarrytown, N.Y., is an elaborate, castlelike Gothic Revival house. Picturesque asymmetry, a variety of foliated windows, tracery and ample verandas typify the mode. (Jack E. Boucher; Lawrence J. Fusaro and Roger Erickson)

windows, tracery and leaded stained glass. House plans were asymmetrical to allow flexibility in arrangement of rooms and to create picturesque external silhouettes. The timely invention of the scroll saw, or jigsaw, and the widespread availability of wood produced that delightful variant known as Carpenter Gothic. More often than not, Carpenter Gothic buildings are sheathed in board-and-batten, whose vertical lines aided and abetted the desired verticality of the style. Grant Wood's famous painting *American Gothic* shows a typical board-and-batten Carpenter Gothic cottage in the background. Lacking authentic models, such domestic Gothic structures, albeit delightful, never achieved the correctness of original medieval examples. However, more elaborate masonry houses, such as Alexander Jackson Davis's masterpiece, Lyndhurst (1838, 1864–65), near Tarrytown, N.Y., aspired to greater Gothic authenticity.

So did Episcopal churches. In June 1859, Philip St. George Cocke, member of a consortium who had recently purchased White Sulphur Springs in western Virginia (now West Virginia), invited Davis to the resort to "select a

The Old State Capitol (1847–49, James H. Dakin; reconstructed 1880–82, William A. Freret), Baton Rouge, La., is one of only two antebellum Gothic state capitols, a style seldom used for government buildings. (David J. Kaminsky)

The Bowen House (c. 1845, Joseph C. Wells), Woodstock, Conn., shows the felicitous combination of Gothic design with frame construction. Board-and-batten siding, seen here, was often employed to give the desired sense of verticality. Even the fence surrounding the yard carries the Gothic theme. (Jack E. Boucher)

Chapel Hall, Gallaudet College (1867–70, Frederick C. Withers), Washington, D.C., is one of the earliest examples of Ruskinian Gothic collegiate architecture in the U.S. Withers continued his Ruskinian Gothic design in the arcaded corridor connecting Chapel Hall (the main building at Gallaudet) with College Hall, built 1875–78. (Ronald Comedy)

Right: Rochester Free Academy (1872–73, A. J. Warner), Rochester, N.Y., illustrates the principles of Ruskinian Gothic. Two kinds of stone trim are set against the red-brick walls for a polychromatic effect. Gothic details in windows, doors and gables are large-scale. (Hans Padelt)

The Syracuse Savings Bank (1875, Joseph Lyman Silsbee), Syracuse, N.Y., shows the effective use of contrasts in color and texture as promulgated by Ruskin. (Jack E. Boucher)

Right: **The Provident Life and Trust Company (1876–79, Frank Furness), Philadelphia, Pa., was obviously an original work but owed a debt to the High Victorian Gothic. (Theodore F. Dillon)**

site and give us the plan of an Episcopal chapel for the place." He reminded the architect that Episcopalians "are wedded to forms to what is established— they like too what is old & English." American church architects, especially when designing Episcopal churches, were strongly influenced by Augustus W. N. Pugin and the English ecclesiologists who vigorously promoted the archeologically accurate Gothic parish church as the only suitable structure for Christian worship.

The Gothic Revival was an enduring style. Post–Civil War Gothic Revivalists were influenced by the writings of English architecture theorist John Ruskin, who advocated the use of contrasting colors of brick and stone to produce bold polychromatic patterns. The Ruskinian or High Victorian Gothic style was eclectic, drawing on Italian and German as well as English Gothic precedents. The style was used mainly for public buildings, including schools, libraries and churches. Such highly personalized work as that of Philadelphia architect Frank Furness reveals the extent to which Gothic forms were adapted to post–Civil War tastes. Furness's work, architectural critic Lewis Mumford once declared, was "bold, unabashed, ugly, and yet somehow healthily pregnant." Buildings such as Philadelphia's Provident Life and Trust Company (1876–79) illustrate what Mumford meant.

Reacting to the excesses of High Victorian Gothic, late-19th-century architects returned to a more imitative Gothic Revival. The Collegiate Gothic that shaped such campuses as Princeton, the University of Pennsylvania and Yale was popular in this period. Gothic also remained the most influential style for churches well into the 20th century and was a great favorite for Period Houses (q.v.).

Romanesque Revival
(Rundbogenstil or Round Arch Style)

Prior to the Civil War, yet another style began to capture the architectural fancy of Americans. This was the Romanesque Revival, also known as the Rundbogenstil or Round Arch style. Its salient characteristic is the rounded arch; not the classical round arch of Roman times, but as filtered through the medieval Romanesque style. Inasmuch as it predated Gothic in Europe, the style was also referred to as Norman. One of the first examples of the early phase of the style, and perhaps the outstanding one, is James Renwick's Smithsonian Institution (1847–51) in Washington, D.C., which in many respects introduced the style to America. The Smithsonian was established by a bequest to the nation from English scientist James Smithson, who directed

Citadel Square Baptist Church (1855–56), Charleston, S.C., is an imposing example of the pre-Richardsonian Romanesque style based on German models. Round arches define the style, as seen in all the openings. Inside, a round-vaulted ceiling carries out the theme. The tower originally culminated in a much taller steeple, which was not replaced after being destroyed in a hurricane. (Charles H. Bayless)

Smithsonian Institution (1847–51, James Renwick), Washington, D.C. One of the seminal buildings of the pre–Civil War Romanesque Revival, the Smithsonian was regarded as heralding the birth of a new American architectural style. The west wing of the seven-part composition seen here appears very ecclesiastical. (Harry H. Lau)

First Evangelical Congregational Church (1851–52, Alexander R. Esty), Cambridge, Mass., recalls New England meeting-house prototypes in its basic form—a rectangle with a projecting tower centering the facade—but the overall feeling and details are quite different. All openings are round-arched, and gable ends have corbelled brick decorations. (George M. Cushing)

simply that it be in Washington and that it be for the "increase and diffusion of knowledge among men." After much debate, Congress accepted the gift in 1846, by which time medieval styles were considered appropriate for educational institutions, particularly because of their association with Oxford and Cambridge universities. Officials of the institution announced an architectural competition, and Renwick, 28 years old at the time, was one among twelve architects who responded. Renwick submitted both a Gothic and a Romanesque Revival design. The latter was selected, and Robert Dale Owen, who had championed the project in Congress, took the occasion to publish a book, *Hints on Public Architecture*, in 1849. In it, he argued that medieval styles were appropriate not only for the Smithsonian, but for other public buildings as well, in great measure because they allowed for more variety than the rigid orders of classical architecture. Owen went on to hope that a new national style of architecture might result. That, of course, never happened. What did happen was a huge influx of Germans to America in the 1840s, architects among them, who popularized the style. German architecture had already been transformed by the Rundbogenstil, and, in fact, Renwick used several German books in designing the Smithsonian.

Not the least attractive feature of the style, especially in comparison to the Gothic Revival, was economy. British architect John Nash once proclaimed

U.S. Soldiers Home, Scott Building (1852–57, Lt. Barton S. Alexander), Washington, D.C. The first major building erected at this institution established by Congress in 1851 is an impressive Romanesque Revival edifice, clothed in white Vermont marble. Almost all of the openings are round-arched. Corbels, employed at salient points, continue the arch motif. (Jack E. Boucher)

that he hated the Gothic style, as "one window costs more trouble than two houses ought to." Not so with Romanesque windows, which seldom contained elaborate, expensive, tracery.

As the style evolved, it was used often for churches, especially those established by and for German Lutheran and Roman Catholic congregations. Surprisingly, nonliturgically oriented Congregationalists also found the style to their liking. In 1844, Richard Upjohn designed that denomination's prestigious Church of the Pilgrims in Brooklyn, N.Y., which met with immediate acclaim. In 1853 the denomination published *A Book of Plans for Churches and Parsonages*, which was intended to promote "convenience, economy, and good taste" in the design of new churches, and which was instrumental in spreading the style across the country. The minister of the Church of the Pilgrims, along with two of its founding members, were on the publication committee. *A Book of Plans* also contained a text, which warned that "voice and sight" (hearing and seeing the minister) could be all too easily lost "mid the labyrinthine intricacies of clustered pillars and groined arches" of the Gothic style. Eschewing such features, the Rundbogenstil espoused others typical of medieval Romanesque design. Most of the 18 designs shown in *A Book of Plans* were in this style, and, in addition to round arches, displayed corbels, chevrons and lozenges. All showed buildings that were smooth in texture, whether built of brick, stone or wood. Not until a later manifestation of the Romanesque, the Richardsonian, would the style be characterized by its ruggedness and craggy texture, and not until then would it be used for residential design to any degree.

Italianate

The architecture of Italy inspired a building style that enjoyed immense popularity beginning in the 1850s and lasting well into the 1880s. Also known as the Tuscan, Lombard, Bracketed and even American style, the Italianate could be as picturesque as the Gothic or as restrained as the Neoclassical. This adaptability made it nearly a national style in the 1850s. Because there are so many variations, some guides distinguish between the Italian Villa style and the Renaissance Revival, even separating the latter into Romano-Tuscan and North Italian modes. While such divisions may be more detailed than necessary, they at least give proof of the enormous popularity and extent of the Italian influence in many guises.

The Patrick Barry House (1857, Gervase Wheeler), Rochester, N.Y., represents the full-blown Italian villa style. Advancing and receding planes, arched window heads, shallow gabled-roof sections supported by a bracketed cornice, not to mention the tower, characterize the type. Wheeler, like Downing and Davis, helped promote the villa style in works such as his *Rural Homes* (1853). (Hans Padelt)

The Main House, James Lick Mill complex (c. 1860), Santa Clara, Calif., is a good example of the Italianate style adapted in wood to a domestic structure. (Jane Lidz)

The Chalfonte Hotel (1875–76, 1879), Cape May, N.J., demonstrates the adaptability of the Italianate to another building type—the summer resort hotel. The Chalfonte is one of many examples of the style that graces one of America's earliest summer resorts. (Jack E. Boucher)

Italianate villa design was borrowed from the rural architecture of northern Italy and introduced by way of England in the late 1830s. Again it was the plans of Alexander Jackson Davis circulated in Andrew Jackson Downing's books that helped popularize the style.

At its most elaborate, the Italianate house had a low roof or roofs (gabled, hipped or both), overhanging eaves with decorative brackets, an entrance tower, round-headed windows (often paired) with hood moldings, corner quoins, arcaded porches and balustraded balconies. Houses with all these

The Reed Building (1885), Wheeling, W. Va., has elaborate second-story window lintels, executed in wood rather than cast iron, and an extremely ornate cornice. (Jack E. Boucher)

Below: **First National Bank Building (1877, P. M. Comegys), Galveston, Tex., is typical of Italianate commercial buildings. The first-floor facade is of cast iron, the second of brick. Capping the building is the requisite heavy, bracketed cornice. (Allen Stross)**

attributes are generally termed Italian villas. At its simplest, the Italianate house could be a square building with low pyramidal roof, bracketed eaves and perhaps a cupola or lantern, or a gable-fronted house with decorative trim embellishing multilevel porches. The latter form was used time and again in summer resort architecture. Both the round-headed windows of Tuscan villas and the classical architraves of Renaissance palaces were frequently used to

The Hart (Hildebrand) Block (1884, Charles D. Meyer), Louisville, Ky., possesses a cast-iron facade that reflects classical treatment. All five floors have slender columns with modified Corinthian capitals. (Jack E. Boucher; C. Alexander)

Below: Asa Packer Mansion (1852), Jim Thorpe, Pa. As befitted his position as the wealthiest man in town, Asa Packer built a prodigious Italian villa that still dominates Jim Thorpe (formerly Mauch Chunk). Elaborate brackets, paired at the corners, add visual and structural support to the overhanging roof slopes, while prominent hoodmolds cover the windows. (Paul Dolinsky, Timothy A. Buehner, Patrick Koby, Sandra Moore, Eric Zehrung)

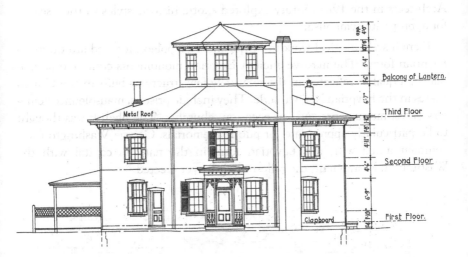

Labels on drawing: Balcony of Lantern, Third Floor, Second Floor, First Floor, Metal Roof, Clapboard

Above: **The Bibb (Octagonal) House (1865), Washington, D.C., shows a house type that flourished in the mid–19th century after the publication of Orson Squire Fowler's** *A Home for All,* **which claimed that the octagon was a far more efficient and space-saving shape than the usual square or rectangle. The unusual form was often embellished with Italianate details. (HABS collection)**

Trinity Union School Church, South Dennis, N.J. This mid-19th-century church has a traditional form, but the segmentally arched windows and paired brackets that decorate the cornice, pediment and tower place it firmly in the Italianate style. (David Ames)

ornament the facades of urban row houses and commercial buildings. Brownstones, the generic name given to close-ordered houses that line the residential streets of many a metropolis, are more often than not Italianate in style. So are many federally sponsored buildings such as customhouses and post offices, especially those designed by Ammi B. Young, who was the supervising architect of the Treasury, the department in charge of governmental construction, from 1852 to 1862.

The development of cast iron and pressed metal technology in the mid–19th century permitted the economical mass production of decorative features that few merchants could have afforded in carved stone. New York City, St. Louis, Portland, Maine, and Portland, Ore., all have districts of cast-iron buildings, and towns across the country still boast stores with cast-iron fronts masquerading as Italian palaces.

Exotic Revivals

Architects in the 19th century explored exotic historic styles in their search for appropriate symbolism.

French archeological work in Egypt under Napoleon focused attention on Egyptian forms. The massive ancient Egyptian monuments connoted permanence, a quality reflected in the relatively few structures built in the United States in the Egyptian Revival style. They include prisons, mausoleums, cemetery gates, monuments and, on occasion, churches. The obelisk was thought to be particularly appropriate for public memorials. George Washington was commemorated with this Egyptian form in the nation's capital with the Washington Monument, the tallest obelisk ever erected.

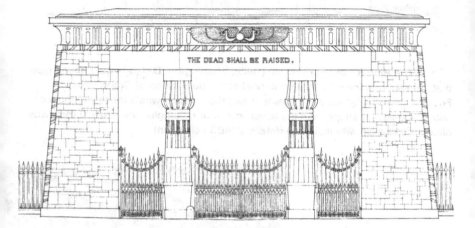

THE DEAD SHALL BE RAISED.

The Grove Street Cemetery Entrance (1845–48, Henry Austin), New Haven, Conn., is an outstanding example of Egyptian Revival architecture of monumental proportions. (A. H. M. Gottschalk)

The Isaac M. Wise Temple (1863–65, James Keyes Wilson), Cincinnati, Ohio, used characteristically intricate surface ornament and minaretlike spires to achieve a Moorish Revival flavor.

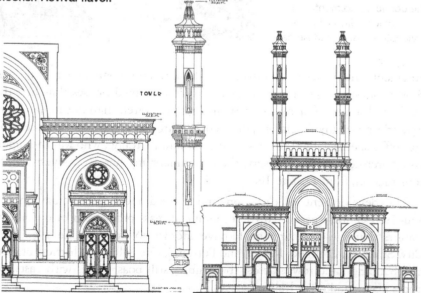

Above: **The First (Downtown) Presbyterian Church (1849–51, William Strickland), Nashville, Tenn., has the battered window and doorframes, concave cornice, winged-disk motif, reeded columns with horizontal bands and palm capitals that appeared on many such Egyptian Revival buildings. (Jack E. Boucher)**

The Ada Theater (1926–27, Frederick C. Hummel), Boise, Idaho. When the theater opened, under the name Egyptian Theatre, the local press rhapsodized that it "embodies the characteristic features of the land of the Nile, from the truncated pyramids which form the great pylons, to the lotus bud pillars with their ornate frescoes." The huge lotus-bud pillars flanking the organ screen were designed after those in Karnak. (Duane Garrett)

Although many 19th-century houses had fashionable "Turkish corners," the use of Near Eastern architectural motifs was rare. A few grand and generally ostentatious houses, such as P. T. Barnum's Bridgeport, Conn., mansion, Iranistan (1847–48), which burned in 1857, sprouted bulbous domes and horseshoe arches, but the Moorish style was most popular for garden structures and such "pleasure palaces" as clubs, hotels and theaters. For quite different reasons, the Moorish Revival also became associated with the Jewish reform movement in America; it distinguished synagogues from churches and had historical precedent in the beautiful Mudejar synagogues of Spain that were built before the 15th century.

On the eve of the Civil War, the United States was a country of diverse interests, cultures and tastes. Nowhere was this diversity seen so clearly as in its architecture, and if the latter half of the 19th century is remembered as the period in which many styles battled for prominence, the seeds of that architectural conflict had already been sown by mid-century.

During the 20th century, exotic buildings continued to be designed and built, primarily in the theatrical realm. Moviegoers sought relief from reality during the Great Depression by watching films in theaters designed to represent oriental palaces, Spanish villages or Egyptian temples. The genre continues to be popular in Las Vegas and Atlantic City, where casinos and hotels such as the Taj Mahal, Caesars Palace and Luxor tell in their very names what particular brand of architectural exoticism they purport to represent.

Debtor's Wing of the Philadelphia County (Moyamensing) Prison (1836, Thomas U. Walter), Philadelphia, Pa., is considered the first archeologically based Egyptian Revival building in the U.S. (Jack E. Boucher)

Laurel Hill Cemetery (1835–36, John Notman), Philadelphia, Pa. A veritable forest of obelisks gives mute testimony to the fondness for Egyptian forms as memorials in American cemeteries. (Jack E. Boucher)

Right: Washington Monument (1848–85, Robert Mills), Washington, D.C., The world's tallest obelisk took over 30 years to build. Architect Mills envisioned a circular "pantheon" around the base, but this was never built, leaving the Egyptian form to remain in isolated splendor. (Robert R. Azola, Dana L. Lockett, Mark Schara)

Fox Theater (1927–29), Mayre, Alger and Vinour), Atlanta, Ga. Exotic Moorish Revival exterior details—onion domes and half-domes, horseshoe arches, loggias and crenellations—embellish this major movie palace, and hint at the exotic splendors to be found within. No wonder the building is known, at least locally, as "The Fabulous Fox." (Jonathan Hillyer)

Loew's Theater (1928–29, John Eberson), Louisville, Ky. This lavish movie palace was decorated in the Churrigueresque mode, the elaborate 18th-century Spanish Baroque style characterized by elaborate and intricate clusters of ornamentation alternating with plain surfaces. Here the decorations are executed in terra cotta with rich, colorful finishes. The theater premiered on Sept. 1, 1928, with the film *Excess Baggage*. One could perhaps say that the building has an excess of architectural baggage. (Jack E. Boucher)

Second Empire

The popularity of the Second Empire style in the 1860s and 1870s reflects the public interest in picturesqueness and asymmetry, characteristics that were introduced to American architecture by the Gothic Revival and Italianate styles and became even more pronounced in the mid- to late 19th century. Architecture of this period, although still usually based on historical precedent, represented a reaction to the stricter historical bent of the earlier revivalists. Mid-century architects reasoned that no age had produced the perfect architectural expression and that they could benefit from all the best of the past. Why hesitate, therefore, to combine features from various styles? Freer adaptation could evoke the spirit of the past without slavish imitation and would allow more creativity. Thus, eclecticism characterized much of the architecture of the immediate post–Civil War period, as did a continued emphasis on the picturesque. Great importance was placed on character and a sense of permanence in buildings. "Delicate" and "beautiful" are adjectives rarely used in describing post–Civil War architecture.

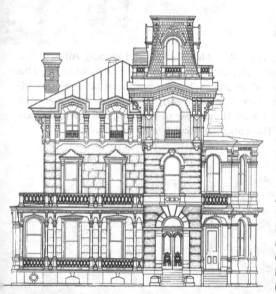

The Goyer-Lee House (1843, 1853, 1873, Edward C. Jones and Mathias H. Baldwin), Memphis, Tenn., is an authoritative statement of the Second Empire style. The brick facade is covered with sandstone veneer and stucco, making it appear more monumental. (Mark P. Frederickson and Darrell K. Pattison)

Below: The Capt. Edward Penniman House (1867–68), Eastham, Mass., proves that even a small, square, one-story house could appear grand with the imaginative addition of a mansard roof. (Cervin Robinson)

Terrace Hill (1867–69, W. W. Boyington), Des Moines, Iowa, is one of the most lavish Second Empire houses in the country. The concrete quoins and window hoods contrast with the red-brick walls. The house now serves as the Iowa governor's mansion. (Robert Thall)

The State, War and Navy (Old Executive Office) Building (1871–88, Alfred B. Mullett), Washington, D.C., is one of the two grandest American public buildings in the Second Empire style; the other is Philadelphia City Hall (1871, John McArthur, Jr.). The State, War and Navy Building has projecting pavilions with superimposed columns, classical pediments and balustrades and a massive mansard roof with two rows of decorative dormers. (Ronald Comedy)

The Second Empire style was borrowed from France. It is named for the reign of Napoleon III (1852–70), who undertook a major building campaign that transformed Paris into a city of grand boulevards and monumental buildings copied throughout Europe and the New World. One of Napoleon's most famous projects was the enlargement of the Louvre (1852–57), which brought back to popularity a roof form developed by 17th-century French Renaissance architect François Mansart.

Above: **The 2300 block of Chapline Street in Wheeling, W. Va., contains several good examples of the Second Empire style in an urban setting. Similar massing, window spacing and unified cornice lines contribute to the homogenous grouping. (Mark L. Hall, Ed Freeman and Richard Cronenberger)**

Lincoln, Nebraska's Old City Hall was built 1874–79 as the city's U. S. Court House and Post Office. Architect Alfred B. Mullett combined elements from several styles, among them Victorian Gothic windows, but capped the building with a prominent dormered mansard roof, the hallmark of the Second Empire style. (David Murphy)

The mansard roof—a double-pitched roof with a steep lower slope—was a hallmark of the Second Empire style. By increasing headroom in the attic space, it provided an additional usable floor. To provide light on this floor, the mansard was almost always pierced with dormers. One of the first major Second Empire–style buildings in America was the Corcoran Gallery (1859–61, James Renwick), Washington, D.C. Confiscated for military use when the Civil War began, the building (now the Renwick Gallery) set the style for many post–Civil War public buildings. In fact, the style became so closely associated with public architecture of the prosperous Grant administration (1869–77) that it is sometimes called the General Grant style. One of its major practitioners was Alfred B. Mullett, who held the office of supervising architect of the Treasury from 1866 to 1874.

Second Empire buildings featured prominent projecting and receding surfaces, often in the form of central and end pavilions. Ornamentation usually included classical pediments (frequently with sculpture groups), balustrades and windows flanked by columns or pilasters. Columns were usually paired and supported entablatures that divided the floors of the building. And there was always the mansard roof. The general effect was monumental and ornate and provided comfortable associations with the latest European building fashion.

Domestic architecture in the Second Empire style is more difficult to characterize, because the mansard roof could be placed on almost any house to create a contemporary look without requiring innovations in plan or ornament.

Above: **Gallatin House (1877, Nathaniel Dudley Goodell), Sacramento, Calif.** This exemplary Second Empire mansion, shown here in a 19th-century print, shared its landscaped grounds with a Second Empire carriage house and an elaborate gazebo. The house served as the California governor's mansion from 1903 until 1967.

Armour-Stiner House, Irvington, N.Y. Sometimes style is not as important as form. This extraordinary octagon was built in 1859–60 and remodeled in the 1870s. The expansive dome, with hip-roofed dormers on each face, provides an overall Second Empire flavor, while the Stick Style (q.v.) is evident in the wall sheathing. The octagonal form, like the Bibb House shown in the chapter on the Italianate style, derives from Orson Squire Fowler's writings. (Thom Laughman)

The interiors were generally elaborations of the Italianate style, with bold plaster cornices and medallions and marble mantels with arched openings.

Although a house with a mansard roof can safely be termed Second Empire regardless of what decorative elements may ornament its facade, other domestic styles in the third quarter of the 19th century—with the exception of the Romanesque Revival—are not so easily distinguished. Many architectural historians lump them together under the term "picturesque eclecticism," and writer John Maass has called it the "nameless period." Domestic architecture of this period freely mixed elements from several styles, and it is sometimes difficult to pinpoint the borrowings.

Stick Style

Evolving out of the Carpenter Gothic, with forays into Swiss chalet territory, the Stick Style flourished in the third quarter of the 19th century. These were the years when summer resorts such as Newport, R.I., and Cape May, N.J., were flourishing, and the general lightness of the style seemed particularly appropriate for houses that were used only during the warmest months, when porches were most needed. Several states erected Stick Style buildings at the Philadelphia Centennial Exposition in 1876, and helped continue the style's popularity a bit longer.

This style of wood construction was characterized by angularity, verticality and asymmetry. Roofs were composed of steep intersecting gables. Verandas and porches were common and were often decorated with simple diagonal braces. In keeping with the idea that architecture should be truthful, the principal characteristic of the Stick Style was the expression of the inner structure of the house through the exterior ornament. As Andrew Jackson Downing put it, somewhat convolutedly, "the main timbers which enter into the frame of a wooden house and support the structure are vertical, and hence the vertical boarding properly signifies to the eye a wooden house." Most often found on gable ends and upper stories, this stick work was usually a series of boards intersecting at right angles and applied over the clapboard surface to symbolize the structural skeleton. Sometimes diagonal boards were incorporated to resemble, or suggest, half-timbering.

The Griswold House (1862–63, Richard Morris Hunt), Newport, R.I., is an elaborate example of the Stick Style. Intersecting boards are superimposed on the clapboard sheathing to suggest the interior framing. All trim is simple and angular. (Jack E. Boucher)

Right: Mark Twain House (1873–74, E. T. Potter and A. H. Thorp), Hartford, Conn., is an amalgam of several styles. Although the house is solidly built of brick and brownstone, its porches, balconies and other wooden trim bespeak the Stick Style. (Jack E. Boucher)

The Dr. Emlen Physick House (1879, Frank Furness), Cape May, N.J., is designed in the Stick Style. The bold design, tapering chimneys, steeply hipped roofs, tall proportions, structural framing overlay and irregular silhouette are typical of Furness's work. (Hugh McCauley)

Hotel, Ocean Grove, N.J. The intricate structure of this triple-decker porch is almost a catalog of Stick Style decoration. The framing that fills the triangular space in front of the gable-ended roof is self-assured and honest, quite the opposite of the sort of decorative jigsaw work employed in Carpenter Gothic ornamentation. (David Ames)

Above, left: The David King House (1871–72), Newport, R.I., has diagonal braces and exposed Stick Style framing. The porch, however, is attached to a mansard-roof house, illustrating how styles were mixed in the post–Civil War period. (Jack E. Boucher)

Queen Anne

The very name of this style suggested eclecticism to its originators. It was coined in England in the late 19th century to describe buildings that supposedly were inspired by the transitional architecture of the pre-Georgian period, when good Queen Anne reigned (1702–14). That had been a time, so the originators of the term claimed, when classical ornament was grafted onto buildings of basically medieval form. The English architect most closely associated with the Queen Anne style was Richard Norman Shaw (1831–1912), whose sprawling manor houses were well known to American architects, having been pictured in many professional architectural publications.

The Long-Waterman House (1889, D. B. Benson), San Diego, Calif., is an all-wood version of the Queen Anne style. Contrast is achieved between the narrow first-floor clapboards and the intricate second-floor shingle patterns. Gables are steep; turrets also provide vertical accents. The encircling veranda has spindlelike ornaments often found on the interior and exterior of Queen Anne houses. (J. Livengood; City of San Diego)

Glenmont (1880, Henry Hudson Holly), West Orange, N.J., the home of Thomas Edison, shows such Queen Anne characteristics as a brick first story contrasted with decorative boarding on the second story, shingles in the gables, a paneled chimney and prominent gables. (Jack E. Boucher)

Above, right: The Ivinson Mansion (1892), Laramie, Wyo., with its verticality, projecting gables, prominent porch, corner bays and turrets, has common Queen Anne features. (Jack E. Boucher)

The Queen Anne style played on contrasting materials. First floors were often brick or stone; upper stories were of stucco, clapboard or decorative shingles, which were used frequently in the United States in place of the tiles popular in England. Huge medieval-type chimneys were common. Roofs were gabled or hipped, often with second-story projections and corner turrets borrowed from French chateaux. Gable ends were ornamented with half-timbering or stylized relief decoration, generally small in scale. Molded or specially shaped bricks were used as decorative accents. Banks of casement windows were common, and upper panes were often outlined with stained-glass squares or clear glass set in small panels. Verandas and balconies opened houses to the outdoors.

Interior plans, which had been moving further and further from classical symmetry, were given even greater freedom. The fully developed Queen Anne plan featured the living hall, a central living and circulation space with both fireplace and grand staircase. This space flowed freely into other ample rooms. Rich, dark woods in wall paneling and beamed ceilings replaced the plaster ornament and bright wallpapers of the Italianate and Second Empire styles.

The first true American Queen Anne building was architect H. H. Richardson's William Watts Sherman House (1874) in Newport, R.I. The informality and amplitude of the Queen Anne style were perfect for the summer "cottages" of Newport, but the style—especially with its prominent (or pretentious) corner turrets—was also the choice of bankers, lawyers, doctors and other professionals who sought to strut their architectural stuff in small-town America in the 1880s and 1890s. They, or their architects, likely learned of the style through *The American Architect and Building News*, the country's first national architectural journal, or other publications that featured Queen Anne designs.

The Col. Walter Gresham House (The Bishop's Palace) (1887–93, Nicholas J. Clayton), Galveston, Tex., has an elaborate tile roof with hips, gables, cones and pyramids corresponding to the articulation of the complex asymmetrical plan. The stonework relates the house to the Richardsonian Romanesque. (Allen Stross)

Right: The house as tower. The O'Dea House was built in 1888 in a newly platted Washington suburb now known as Berwyn Heights, Prince George's County, Md. The facade is overwhelmed by a three-story tower, fronted on the first floor by a wraparound porch. In a feature typical of the Queen Anne style, sheathing is varied: first-floor walls are clad with plain board siding, those above with scalloped and fish-scale shingles. (Jack E. Boucher)

The Queen Anne style also changed urban row-house architecture. The projecting bay front topped by a gable or pinnacle roof was found in cities from Boston to San Francisco in the 1880s. Decorative brick patterns, molded bricks and colorful stained-glass transoms enlivened the facades of these row houses. Similar features were found in small commercial buildings of the 1880s and 1890s, but the picturesque effects of the Queen Anne style were employed to best advantage in substantial free-standing residences. With time, the Queen Anne became tamer, and as the 20th century progressed, it merged with little fanfare into the Colonial Revival. Then, at the end of the 20th century, the style reappeared in full force in upscale housing developments. Vinyl siding in many patterns, however, has replaced the wooden clapboards and shingles of the 19th-century houses, while the "great room" has replaced the living hall as the major interior space.

Shingle Style

An American style that evolved out of the Queen Anne was the Shingle Style. It was born in New England, where the fondness for natural wood shingles reflected post-Centennial interest in American colonial architecture, especially the shingle architecture of the coastal towns that were being rediscovered as fashionable resorts. The reappearance of the gambrel roof in some Shingle Style structures was also a result of this antiquarian interest.

The William G. Low House (1887, McKim, Mead and White), Bristol, R.I., was one of the nation's great Shingle Style monuments. A myriad of window forms, an ample veranda and projecting bays were all controlled by the simple roof and the shingle covering.

The Isaac Bell House (Edna Villa) (1882–83, McKim, Mead and White), Newport, R.I., has a relatively calm silhouette and a distinctive horizontal massing. The shingle covering unifies the somewhat disparate massing of the windows. (Thomas B. Schubert)

The Sea Cliff Inn (1886), Nantucket, Mass., was a typical Shingle Style hotel, a style closely associated with northeastern resort architecture. Both the shingle covering and the Palladian windows in the gables indicated renewed interest in American colonial architecture. (Jack E. Boucher)

Although many Shingle Style buildings fall somewhere along the line of evolution from the Queen Anne, the first examples of the fully developed style appeared in the 1880s. Actually, the style was not named until the mid-20th century, by architectural historian Vincent Scully. Among the important practitioners of the style were architects Willis Polk in the West and H. H. Richardson, Bruce Price, William Ralph Emerson, John Calvin Stevens and McKim, Mead and White in the East. There are few Southern examples of the style, which was overwhelmingly residential, rather than commercial, in expression.

Shingle Style buildings were tamer and more horizontal than their Queen Anne predecessors. The lasting impression, especially in comparison with Queen Anne buildings, is one of relative calm. Ornament was greatly reduced, and there was also less diversity in texture. Roofs continued to be prominent and complex, but dormers, when they appeared, were often hipped or eyebrow rather than gabled. Circular turrets and verandas remained popular but were integrated more fully into the overall design. Sometimes the roof extended down from the ridge in a single run to cover an expansive veranda. The veranda opened through many entrances into the house, where the plan continued the Queen Anne trend toward openness and informality. Most important, the entire building was usually covered with wooden shingles. When a contrasting material was used, as for porch columns and foundations, it was often rough-surfaced, coursed stone or fieldstone rubble, which complemented the rough natural texture of the shingles. The emphasis of the Shingle Style was on the surface—the shingled skin that covered the frame and unified all parts of the building. This was the exact opposite of the Stick Style, which sought to display the skeleton, or frame of the building. Still, it is the overall effect, not the material, that truly defines the Shingle Style.

Barnegat Lifesaving Station, Barnegat, N.J. This delightful little structure bridges the gap between the Queen Anne and the Shingle Style. The octagonal tower bespeaks the former, while the otherwise horizontal mass of the composition, informal fenestration and—of course—the shingle cladding, reflect the latter. (David Ames)

Richardsonian Romanesque

In only a few instances has an American architectural style been so influenced by one figure as to bear that person's name. But so it was with Henry Hobson Richardson (1838–86) and the late-19th-century Romanesque Revival. Whereas the earlier, pre–Civil War manifestation of the style had been based largely on German sources, the Romanesque of the 1870s and 1880s drew on Spanish and southern French influences. Even so, under Richardson's aegis, it became a uniquely American style. Still present were the round arches framing window and door openings (usually minus chevrons and lozenges), but gone were vertical silhouettes and smooth stone or brick facings. Richardson's buildings were more horizontal and rough in texture. Heaviness was an ever-present characteristic of the style—emphasized not only by the stone construction but also by deep window reveals, cavernous door openings and, occasionally, bands of windows. These openings were often further defined by a contrasting color or texture of stone or by short, robust columns. Bainbridge Bunting, in his *Houses of Boston's Back Bay* (Belknap Press, Cambridge, Mass., 1967), provided a superb shorthand insight on Richardsonian Romanesque when he stated that it was "characterized by a mood that is best described as gloomy robustness."

The John J. Glessner House (1885–87, H. H. Richardson), Chicago, Ill., is one of the architect's finest houses. It shows simple massing and inherent patterns of coursed masonry used effectively for ornamental effect. (Eric N. Delony; Cervin Robinson)

Union Station (1900), Nashville, Tenn., indicates the style's long popularity. The building's debt to Richardson is obvious in the rock-faced masonry, round arches, soaring tower and general massiveness. (Jack E. Boucher)

The Inner Quad Arcade (1891, Shepley, Rutan and Collidge), Stanford University, Stanford, Calif., combines Richardsonian masonry with a rhythmic arcade suggestive of the California missions. The complex was designed by the successor firm to Richardson's and succeeded in accomplishing the donor's request that the buildings have a distinctly California flavor. (Jack E. Boucher)

As with the preceding Romanesque revival, Richardsonian Romanesque was favored for churches, university buildings, and public structures such as railroad stations, city halls and courthouses. Consequently, impressive towers were often part of the design. In the best examples, a single tower, massive and bold in outline, crowns the ensemble.

Wayne County Court House (1890–93, James McLaughlin), Richmond, Ind., is a good example of the many Richardsonian Romanesque courthouses built throughout the country in the late 19th century. Their powerful masonry masses suggest the majesty of the law. The recessed loggia above the entrance gave a touch of relief from the heavy masonry facade and allowed the stonemasons a chance to display their talents. (Jack E. Boucher)

Just as one architect was responsible for the style, one building established its popularity. Richardson's 1872 design for Trinity Church in Boston won one of the most prestigious architectural competitions of the day. Although it is more revivalistic than some of his later structures, Trinity has a massiveness and disposition of parts that is uniquely Richardsonian. Another Richardson design, Pittsburgh's Allegheny County Courthouse and Jail (1884–88), had perhaps even more influence. In many West Virginia and Ohio cities downstream on the Ohio River from Pittsburgh, as well as in towns and cities farther west, county courthouses can be found that are patterned after this building. Especially after Richardson's premature death in 1886, admiring architects adopted his style for schools, post offices and commercial and federal buildings across the country. Again, the office of supervising architect of the Treasury helped spread the style across the nation, especially during the short but prolific terms of James H. Windrim (1889–91) and Willoughby J. Edbrooke (1891–93).

Riley Row (1887, Wilcox and Johnston), St. Paul, Minn., has the rough stone trim, squat columns and arched openings found on many late-19th-century Richardsonian Romanesque row houses. (Jack E. Boucher)

Trinity Episcopal Church (1872–77, H. H. Richardson), Boston, Mass. More than any structure in the history of American architecture, this building established a style—and an architect. The central tower is modeled on the old cathedral in Salamanca, Spain. Strength is expressed in huge blocks of rock-faced granite, with accents of red sandstone. The porch, a later addition by the architect's successor firm, presents a more florid Romanesque countenance than the building it fronts. (Jack E. Boucher)

Although Richardson produced relatively few houses in the Romanesque style (he is also noted for his Queen Anne and Shingle Style designs), there were enough to inspire a plethora of followers. A large house was required to support the massive stoniness of the Romanesque style, but elements of Richardson's work—such as broad round arches, squat columns, eyebrow dormers and carved, intertwining floral details—found their way into the vocabulary of many local builders. Numerous masonry row houses still exist to pay tribute to Richardson's creativity and immense popularity.

Allegheny County Courthouse and Jail (1884–86, H. H. Richardson), Pittsburgh, Pa. When he was told he would not live much longer, Richardson wrote, "Let me have time to finish Pittsburgh and I should be content without another day." He was referring to this commission, which remains one of his masterworks. This close-up view of the roofline shows massive components coupled with careful attention to detail, characteristics of the best of his work. (Jack E. Boucher)

Bank of Wheeling (1892, Edward Bates Franzheim), Wheeling, W. Va. A cavernous arch, supported by squat columns, spanned almost the full width of the first-floor entrance of this bank. Arches and columns diminished in scale on the two upper stories. This fine example of the Richardsonian Romanesque style was demolished in 1983. (Mark L. Hall)

Rustic

Rustic is one of the most easily identified of all architectural styles. Drawing inspiration from a number of sources, it reached its pinnacle during the first half of the 20th century. Although prime examples are found in state and national parks throughout the country, there are many privately constructed buildings in the style as well.

Shelter House (1849), Cave Hill Cemetery, Louisville, Ky. Originally the cemetery office, this rare pre–Civil War example of Rustic design resembles structures in A. J. Downing's 1841 publication, *Landscape Gardening*. Bark is used for exterior sheathing, while some, but not all, of the diagonal braces of the portico seem to be trying to imitate ogee arches, often found in Gothic Revival design. The Rustic style of the shelter complements the informal, "romantic" layout of the cemetery itself. (Jack E. Boucher)

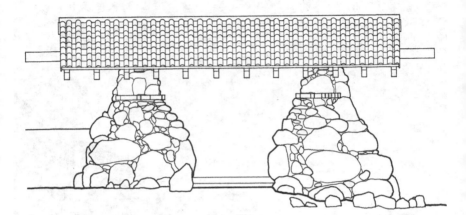

Oaklawn Avenue Waiting Station (1906, Charles and Henry Greene), South Pasadena, Calif. Rarely have riders been treated so aesthetically in American architecture. Built to shelter passengers waiting for trolleys on the Pacific Electric Line, this Rustic station combines boulders, brick, redwood and red tile in its makeup. The station helped set the tone for the neighborhood, which the brothers Greene embellished with stylish Craftsman-style houses (Bungalows, q.v.). (Todd Skenderian)

Multnomah Falls Lodge (1925, A. E. Doyle), Historic Columbia River Highway, Troutdale vicinity, Ore. Natural materials—split fieldstone walls and cedar-shingled roof—and an informal layout help relate this Rustic lodge to its scenic surroundings. The steep slope of the roof echoes the steep hillside behind, where Multnomah Falls can be seen. The lodge was built as an adjunct to the Columbia River Highway, begun in 1913 as one of the first scenic highways in the nation. (Brian Grogan for HAER)

Timberline Lodge (1936–37, U. S. Forest Service architects), Mount Hood National Forest, Ore. So "at home" in the Cascade Range is this Rustic-style lodge that it has been termed "Cascadian" in style. Built as a WPA (Works Progress Administration) effort during the Depression, the building seems to rise from a field of boulders *(above)*. The steep rooflines echo the slopes of the surrounding mountains, though some suggest they also recall the forms of traditional teepees. Exposed eave ends are carved as buffalo and bear heads *(below)*. (Marvin Rand)

Andrew Jackson Downing, America's first landscape architect of note, can be credited with cultivating the style in its infancy, suggesting in his many writings that structures based on nature were the perfect accouterments to landscape design. For shelters, he suggested unpeeled logs as supports, and thatch, or bark, as suitable roofing materials. In a rocky landscape, he used boulders for walls and chimneys, always stressing that "rocks must be arranged in a natural manner, avoiding all regularity and appearance of formal art." The step from rustic shelters and cabins to rustic lodges was a short one, based more on differences of scale than basic philosophy. The great Adirondack summer camps that dotted northern New York state at the turn of the 20th century took the rustic ethic and ran with it. These comprised a great number and variety of individual structures, or cabins, which were generally of log construction, and were built to serve specific functions, from dining to entertainment, from sleeping to storage. Some were small, some were huge. All were built on stone foundations, and most were sited to fit as naturally as possible into the landscape, taking advantage of mountain vistas or lakeside views. Rooflines were often exaggerated in their steepness, not only to help shed the heavy snows of winter, but to echo natural forms and to reflect the silhouettes of the ever-present mountains. Logs often extended far beyond corner notches to emphasize their natural forms. Porches, with railings of unpeeled timbers and log "columns," were equipped with rustic rocking chairs and swings. Because summers in the great north woods were cool, large fireplaces were needed for warmth on long evenings. Huge chimneys built of boulders laid as naturally as possible were a common feature. Inside, fireplace "mantels" were generally large stone slabs, spanning cavernous openings. The informality of design and arrangement of spaces in the rustic mode was not unlike contemporary work in the Shingle Style. More than in most styles, furnishings were designed and constructed to accord with the building.

Clock (1919), Paradise Inn, Mt. Rainier National Park, Wash. This enormous tall-case, or grandfather, clock presides over the lobby of the Rustic-style inn. Fabricated of polished Alaskan cedar by a German craftsman, it stands 14 feet 2 inches tall. Grandfather would have to stand on a ladder—Rustic of course—if he ever needed to adjust the hands of the clock face. (Jack E. Boucher)

Chateau (1932–34), Oregon Caves National Monument, Ore. Fitted into a natural ravine, this Rustic structure is sided with cedar-bark veneer, applied vertically. It and other buildings in the Oregon Caves complex are surrounded by naturalistic landscaping, planted by CCC workers from 1934 to 1941. (Patrick B. Guthrie)

Burntside Lodge, Cabin #27 (early 1930s), Ely Vicinity, Minn. This Rustic resort/retreat camp consists of a main lodge and a number of cabins. Typical of many log buildings of its type, Cabin #27 has log ends that project far beyond the saddle notches to enhance the Rustic look and feel. Although they are somewhat protected by the overhanging eaves, these exposed log ends are definitely more picturesque than practical. (Jet Lowe)

The Adirondack camps were, of course, private facilities, but some of the greatest examples of the Rustic style were built for the public, primarily in national parks such as Yellowstone, Grand Canyon and Yosemite. Old Faithful Inn at Yellowstone, dating from 1903–04, has a seven-story lobby that recalls natural forms with an astonishing array of gnarled logs and railings. During the Depression, the National Park Service assisted a number of states in designing and building facilities in state parks. These were constructed largely by members of the Civilian Conservation Corps (CCC), working under the supervision of so-called LEMs (locally experienced men), who insured that construction was in accord with local traditions. The facilities were designed to provide the general public, especially families, opportunities to coexist with nature—even if nature in the parks was largely manmade. Of course, families also coexisted with other families. For the most part, cabins were clustered in groups or camps, while a larger log or stone structure served as park headquarters and supply store. Outdoor fireplaces allowed city dwellers to try their hand at grilling. So prevalent was the style in these parks that it is sometimes referred to as "parkitecture," or "government rustic." Although the Rustic style seems to have run its course for now, the best examples that remain are well loved, well tended and well used. So popular are these Depression-era cabins in some state parks that lotteries are held to select occupants, who are usually restricted in their lengths of stay. As America moves farther and farther away from its early beginnings and natural roots, the style seems to be more and more appreciated; perhaps it is ripe for a revival.

Beaux-Arts

Les beaux-arts—the fine arts—refers essentially to the aesthetic principles enunciated and perpetuated by the École des Beaux-Arts in France. The École was established in the Napoleonic era as the successor to the part of the French Académie that was founded in the 17th century to monitor painting, sculpture and architecture. The doctrines and teaching techniques of the École dominated French architecture until the 20th century. Therefore, the Beaux-Arts tradition spans a period of more than 250 years and includes designs as diverse as the officially sanctioned east facade of the Louvre (1667–70) and the Paris Opéra (1861–74). Stylistically, it is almost impossible to use the same words to describe the calm, horizontal, elegant, rhythmic east facade of the Louvre and the exuberant, wedding-cake Opéra. The latter, more than any other French structure, epitomizes the Second Empire style and exemplifies the *horror vacui*—an abhorrence of undecorated surface areas—that is characteristic of one phase of the Beaux-Arts tradition.

The A. C. Bliss House (1907, A. Goenner), Washington, D.C., proves that the Beaux-Arts style was an amalgam—here mixing Roman quoins, an oversized late Renaissance dormer with a broken pediment and an exaggerated, steep roof that shows late medieval French influence. (Jack E. Boucher)

The Tremaine-Gallagher House (c. 1914, F. W. Striebinger), Cleveland Heights, Ohio, is a domestic-scale example of the late Beaux-Arts style, which was characterized by a quiet elegance suited to a large suburban mansion such as this. (Martin Linsey)

Whitehall (1900–02, Carrère and Hastings), Palm Beach, Fla., has a monumental main stair whose bronze balustrade is complemented by the ornate furnishings. (Jack E. Boucher)

The Library of Congress (1889–97, Smithmeyer and Pelz), Washington, D.C., is one of America's most grandiose Beaux-Arts designs. Nearly every element of the style is found here, including the monumental entrance stairway. (Jack E. Boucher)

The City of Paris Dry Goods Company (1896, Clinton Day; reconstructed 1908–09, James R. Miller), San Francisco, Calif., was an early Beaux-Arts commercial structure. This detail shows an Art Nouveau influence appropriate to its name. (Robert Freed)

The American architects who were trained in Paris at the École or by other American architects who had studied there are legion. Starting with Richard Morris Hunt, who in 1846 was the first American to attend the École, and H. H. Richardson, the second, a partial list includes Louis Sullivan, John Stewardson, Bernard Maybeck, Addison Mizner, Julia Morgan, Ernest Flagg, John Mervin Carrère and Thomas Hastings. All were influenced by the academic design principles of the École, which emphasized the study of Greek and Roman structures, composition and symmetry, accompanied by elaborate two-dimensional wash or watercolor renderings of the buildings.

As in Europe, American Beaux-Arts designs were generally for colossal public buildings, memorials or urban landscapes. Many of the great exhibitions, such as those held in Philadelphia (1876), Chicago (1893) and St. Louis (1904), displayed Beaux-Arts compositions of phenomenal complexity that had a great impact on the public. Admittedly, these mostly temporary buildings were of plaster, rather than stone or marble, making their complexity and ambition more understandable, and certainly more affordable. This phase of the Beaux-Arts tradition is well represented in the United States by the exuberant design for Memorial Hall (1875–76, Hermann J. Schwarzmann) at the Centennial Exposition in Philadelphia. Memorial Hall has huge sculptural groups animating its skyline, another distinguishing characteristic of the style. Plans of such buildings are rigidly formal and

Kykuit (1911–13, Delano and Aldrich), Pocantico Hills, N.Y. John D. Rockefeller, Sr., commissioned the same New York architects who had designed his chateauesque house in 1902–05 to remodel it in the Beaux-Arts manner a decade later. The studied symmetry, plentiful quoins and an elaborately decorated pediment are typical Beaux-Arts features.

Meridian Hill Park (1930, Horace Peaslee), Washington, D.C. The cascade, a "water staircase," is the centerpiece of this Beaux-Arts park. Water from jets that front a triumphal arch at the top spills into thirteen basins before flowing into the reflecting pool. (Jack E. Boucher)

Bancroft Hall, U. S. Naval Academy, Annapolis, Md. Dating from the first decade of the 20th century, Bancroft Hall, the midshipmen's residence, is one of the centerpieces of architect Ernest Flagg's Beaux-Arts conception for the U. S. Naval Academy. The rotunda, with its imposing vistas, axial stairway, elaborate decorations, and arches supported by classical columns and pilasters, is one of its most impressive spaces. (Jet Lowe)

axial. A later example of the style as applied to a monumental structure is Grand Central Terminal (1903–13, Reed and Stem; Warren and Wetmore) in New York City.

Near the end of the century, however, such designs—with their heavy ashlar stone bases, grand stairways, paired columns with plinths, monumental attics, grand arched openings, cartouches, and decorative swags—gave way to more sedate forms, which were used for the town houses and the country and resort villas of the rich.

Monument Terrace (1924–25, Aubrey Chesterman), Lynchburg, Va. This Beaux-Arts stairway, leading to an 1850s Greek Revival courthouse, was built as a World War I memorial. Ornamental paving patterns, stone balusters, baroque scrolls and urns decorate the stairway, which has become the city's architectural symbol. (Richard Cheek)

Hudson County Courthouse (1906–10, Hugh Roberts), Jersey City, N.J. Before it was demolished, this huge building was one of the state's best examples of the Beaux-Arts style. The central hall, open from the first floor to the roof, and lit by a stained-glass skylight, contained marble balustrades and columns. Winged allegorical figures embellished the pendentives below the saucer dome. (Jack E. Boucher)

B&O Railroad Company Headquarters Building (1904–06, Parker, Thomas & Rice), Baltimore, Md. The B&O embellished its home city with a steel-framed office building that contained many avant-garde conveniences. Architecturally, however, the Beaux-Arts entrance harkened back to antiquity. Above a grandiose arch framing the door, a statue of the Roman god Mercury (representing commerce) perches to the left of a globe, while an allegorical figure (Progress of Industry) is on the right. (James W. Rosenthal)

Classical Revival

The later, more refined state of the Beaux-Arts tradition influenced the American Classical Revival, which was popular during the first half of the 20th century. This style is sometimes termed Neoclassical Revival, and is related to the early-19th-century Neoclassical style. Stone, especially marble and smooth-faced limestone ashlar, was a favorite facing material. Federal government buildings owed much to the Beaux-Arts interpretation of classical design, especially after the passage of the Tarsney Act, introduced by Missouri Congressman John C. Tarsney, in 1893. In the words of *The American Architect and Building News* (25 February 1893), the act was "the first to take the public architecture out of the Government plan-factory and submit it to the best professional men in the country." In short, government buildings could now be designed as the result of architectural competitions, not only by the supervising architect of the Treasury. In part inspired by the classical architecture of the 1893 World's Fair in Chicago, the Tarsney Act was not immediately implemented, but by 1903, when James Knox Taylor, who held the post of supervising architect from 1897 to 1912, decreed "we will construct buildings of the classic style of architecture, as the old Greeks and Romans did," the Romanesque hegemony that had prevailed in designs emanating from his office had become a thing of the past.

The Cannon Office Building (1908, Carrère and Hastings) of the House of Representatives, with its calm composition of giant columns on an ashlar base and arched fenestration, is a reflection of Perrault's design for the east facade of the Louvre. No matter how Roman the Jefferson Memorial may appear at first sight, the fact that its architect, John Russell Pope, studied at the École (as did Carrère and Hastings) suggests that the 20th-century Classical Revival in the United States was the child of the Beaux-Arts tradition more than of the ancient Mediterranean world.

The Cannon House Office Building (1908, Carrère and Hastings), Washington, D.C., with its monumental size, grand entrance stairs, rusticated podium and arched first-floor windows, typifies the late Classical Revival style, which was especially popular for government buildings and monuments, particularly in the nation's capital. (Jack E. Boucher)

Lynchburg National Bank (1915–16, Alfred C. Bossom), Lynchburg, Va., shows the careful attention paid to the siting of Classical Revival buildings. Both elevations of this corner building are important and, while obviously related to each other, are subtly different. (Richard Cheek)

In the late 19th and early 20th centuries, commissions for public buildings and grand houses of industrial moguls went to architects trained in the Beaux-Arts tradition. These architects generally produced academic designs based on classical or Renaissance precedents.

The tradition of academic revivals also included Gothic, Tudor, Georgian and Spanish colonial styles, all of which enjoyed great popularity from the 1890s through the 1930s. During this same period, however, structures were built that were not inspired by styles of the past. It was these structures, rather than their more popular contemporaries, that heralded the course of 20th-century architecture.

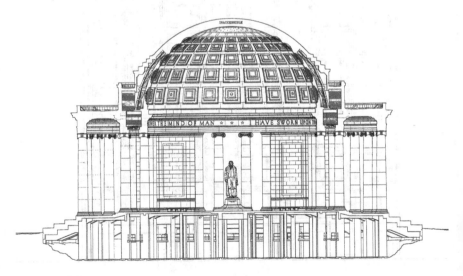

Jefferson Memorial (1937–43, John Russell Pope), Washington, D.C. Based on the Roman Pantheon, the memorial incorporates architecture, sculpture, and inscriptions to convey its message. This drawing is a transverse section through the building. (Amy L. Darling, Ellyn P. Goldkind, Lynn E. Holler, Dana L. Lockett, Mark Schara, Jose Raul Vazquez)

Chicago School

Chicago is the city most associated with development of the tall commercial building. Although earlier Chicago commercial architecture built on advances made elsewhere, most notably in Philadelphia and New York, it was in that Midwestern city in the last quarter of the 19th century that new technology and materials were exploited by innovative architects and engineers to produce the skeleton-framed skyscraper that would transform cities around the world.

The Republic Building (1903–05, 1909, Holabird and Roche), Chicago, Ill., with its banks of Chicago windows and extremely delicate-seeming structure, is the work of a firm that produced some of the most starkly functional buildings of the Chicago School. (Skidmore, Owings and Merrill)

The Ayer Building (1900, Holabird and Roche), Chicago, Ill., clearly reflects its steel frame in the grid pattern of the facade; the walls are composed almost entirely of windows. No superfluous ornament mars the clean lines of the horizontal terra-cotta spandrels. (Cervin Robinson)

The commercial architecture of the Chicago School was the result of important advances in construction technology. Building height had been limited by the massiveness of masonry walls needed for support, even after the invention of the passenger elevator made upper stories easily accessible. Numerous architects experimented with the use of cast- and wrought-iron members to carry the weight of interior floors, but it was not until construction began on the Home Life Building (1883–85, William Le Baron Jenney), that a complete iron and steel skeleton was first used. Combined with improvements in fireproofing, wind bracing and foundation technology, the skeleton frame made tall buildings possible.

A commercial building in the Chicago School style was tall in comparison to its predecessors—usually more than 6 stories but fewer than 20. It was rectangular, with a flat roof and terminating cornice. Ornamentation was usually minimal and subordinated to the functional expression of the internal skeleton that appeared as a grid of intersecting piers and horizontal spandrels. Because the exterior walls of a skeleton-framed structure do not have to bear tremen-

Above, below, and right: **The Reliance Building** (1890, 1894, Burnham and Root), Chicago, Ill., took advantage of the steel skeletal frame to display large areas of glass, with extraordinary detailing on the terra-cotta spandrels. The projecting oriel windows give the building a soaring quality. (Cervin Robinson)

dous weights, they can have large areas of glass, terra cotta or other nonsupporting materials. Windows filled a great proportion of the wall space. Two types of windows were particularly characteristic of the commercial style. One was the projecting bay or oriel that ran the full height of the building, emphasizing the verticality. The other was the so-called Chicago window, composed of a large fixed central pane flanked by two narrow casements that opened to provide ventilation. Large display windows usually occupied the ground-floor level. Above were floors of identical office space. Facades were organized in a number of ways. Some borrowed minor elements of Richardsonian Romanesque or Gothic Revival ornament. The buildings that were more stark and devoid of ornament appear the most modern, for they presaged the mid-20th-century development of glass and steel skyscrapers.

The architect who developed the best-known and most distinctive architectural treatment for tall commercial buildings was Louis Sullivan. His buildings, like a classical column, had a base consisting of the lower two stories, a main shaft in which verticality was emphasized by piers between the windows (occasionally joined by arcading at the top) and—the crowning glory—an elaborate and boldly projecting terra-cotta cornice. Besides this basic organi-

Above and right: **The Prudential (Guaranty) Building (1894–95, Adler and Sullivan), Buffalo, N.Y., illustrates the early formula for high-rise construction, which divided a building into three parts: a base, a shaft housing identical floors of offices and an elaborate cornice crowning the composition. The elaborate detailing is typically Sullivanesque.** (Jack E. Boucher)

zation, Sullivan's buildings can easily be identified by their distinctive low-relief ornament of intricately interwoven foliate designs. This remarkably creative ornamentation usually appeared at the entrance (often an arch), on the spandrels and on the cornice.

Along with Jenney and Sullivan, important names in the development of the tall commercial building include Daniel H. Burnham, John Wellborn Root, William Holabird, Martin Roche and Dankmar Adler, Sullivan's part-

ner. A number of people associated with prominent Chicago architectural firms also had engineering experience, which helped account for the surge of creative structural advances emanating from the city between 1875 and 1900. Although the structural techniques of the Chicago School spread throughout the country, its stripped, no-nonsense exterior design—in many cases, an extremely personal architectural expression—succumbed to the triumphant academicism of the Beaux-Arts–trained eastern architects who were largely responsible for the 1893 World's Columbian Exposition in Chicago. However, significant buildings of the Chicago School appeared in many parts of the United States until World War I; the Colcord Building (1910, Robinson and Sheridan) in Oklahoma City, Okla., is a notable example.

Bungalows

The word "bungalow" can be traced to India, where it was used by the British in the 19th century to designate a house type that was one story high and had large, encircling porches. That they were especially prominent in Bengal may be gathered from the fact that the word derives from the adjective *bangla,* meaning "belonging to Bengal." In California the term was applied to houses that, while having the same characteristics of a single story with a porch or porches, owed far more to other antecedents than to anything specifically Indian. Among the immediate ancestors of what came to be known as the California bungalow were the typical small-scale, one-story, Queen Anne–style cottages that had been built in such profusion throughout the state in the 1880s and 1890s. To this basic form architects brought elements of the Craftsman movement, the Stick Style and—in some instances—even a Japanese flavor to produce a distinctly American synthesis.

In the best examples, bungalows display a fine degree of craftsmanship and are constructed of materials left as close as possible to their natural state. Cobblestones, with their rounded shapes prominently displayed, were laid up in foundations and chimneys; walls, whether frame or shingle, were stained a natural shade of brown; and roofs, with their wide overhangs displaying exposed rafters or knee braces, were often of shingle. When the walls were stuccoed, the roof would more than likely be of tile. In the worst examples, bungalows tended to be ill-designed and hastily built, and the pejorative term "bungaloid" came into being.

In 1909, in his *Craftsman Homes,* Gustav Stickley sought to tell what the style was all about, declaring that a bungalow was "a house reduced to its simplest form," one that "never fails to harmonize with its surroundings, because its low, broad proportions and absolute lack of ornamentation give it a char-

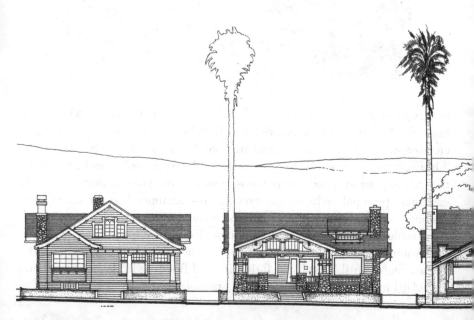

acter so natural and unaffected that it seems to sing into and blend with any landscape." Stickley further lauded the type by stating that it could "be built of any local material and with the aid of such help as local workmen can afford, so it is never expensive unless elaborated out of all kinship with its real character of a primitive dwelling. It is beautiful, because it is planned and built to meet simple needs in the simplest and most direct way." Or, as Fred Thompson, in his *Practical Bungalows for Town and Country* (Frederick J. Drake & Co., Chicago, 1916), had it, "there is nothing either affected or insincere about these little houses. They are neither consciously artistic nor consciously rustic. They are the simple and unconscious expression of the needs of their owners, and as such they can be credited with the best kind of architectural propriety." He added: "Higher than two stories they do not soar."

Sears, Roebuck agreed with Stickley and Thompson and did its part to spread the bungalow gospel by offering a plethora of models in its mail-order catalogs. Sears agreed with Stickley's concept of having local workers construct the bungalows, but it differed from him in the matter of materials. Precut lumber, nails, doors and other components were shipped to the site. Thanks to Sears and other building-supply companies, the style spread across the country, and regional variations became few and far between.

As befitted the exterior appearance, the bungalow interior, both in plan and detail, was also forthright, direct and functional. Front doors opened directly into living rooms, which were often, in turn, directly connected to the dining room or dining area. In many instances the two spaces were separated

The Martin Avenue bungalows, Hanchett Residence Park (1910s), San Jose, Calif., are all individual in design, yet they display salient characteristics of the style and relate to each other in overall massing, scale and texture. (Barbara Friedman and John Murphy)

The Irwin House (1906, Greene and Greene), Pasadena, Calif., is one of the architects' masterpieces. In some respects a bungalow on a large scale, it rests on a stone terrace composed of natural boulders. Splayed eaves and strong horizontal lines established by the balconies give the house a decidedly Japanese flavor. (Ralston H. Nagata)

only by a half wall. A major element of the interior was the living-room fireplace, emphasized by cobblestones or clinker bricks. Ceilings were often beamed, at least in the major rooms, and all wooden surfaces were finished in natural stains. But if the hearth was the center of the house in winter, in summer the bungalow stretched to the out-of-doors. Glass doors led to porches or terraces that were often covered with pergolas supporting vines.

Furnishings often went hand-in-hand with bungalows, as the mention of Gustav Stickley would indicate. Craftsman-style furnishings, with their straight, honest lines and natural wood finishes, most often of oak, and more often than not of golden oak, were the perfect complement. Thompson noted the correlation of house and furniture by declaring that "if the California bungalow is plastered, the millwork which is added is of the simplest character, and generally follows the straight lines of the Mission furniture."

The bungalow style reached its apogee early in its history, in the work of the brothers Charles S. and Henry M. Greene of Pasadena. Their style transcended the basic bungalow form, however, and it cannot be said that they followed Stickley's dictum of meeting "simple needs in the simplest and most direct way." The Craftsman tradition, always a part of the bungalow ethic, found its highest expression in their work. The "woodenness" of construction was not only expressed but also emphasized with elegant joinery; beams were not only exposed but also rounded or cut at the angle that would best express both function and beauty. In the work of the Greenes, the bungalow became the western equivalent of the contemporary Prairie Style (q.v.) then being adopted in the middle sections of the country.

The Longview Farm office (1914, Henry Ford Hoit), Lee's Summit, Mo., shows many affinities with the bungalow style, including a pergola that eases the transition between the building and the out-of-doors. (David J. Kaminsky)

The Melville Klauber House (1908–09, Irving J. Gill), San Diego, Calif., has Craftsman-style interior features like those adopted in many bungalows, notably the predominance of natural woods. (Marvin Rand)

This Benicia, Calif., cottage is typical of many built in California in the 1880s and 1890s. Its irregular plan and elaborate decorative elements seem Queen Anne, but its small size, prominent porch and shallow pitched gables are forerunners of the Bungalow style. (Sirlin Studios)

Jimmy Carter Boyhood Home (1922), Plains vicinity, Ga. This bungalow has an expansive, low-pitched roof that extends to cover a broad, screened, front porch. President Carter spent his formative years here, from age four until he left to attend the U. S. Naval Academy. (Dana Peak and Jason Breyer)

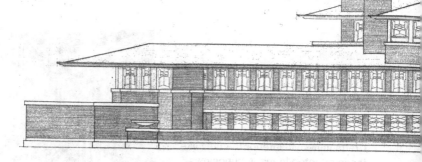

Prairie Style

In 1912, in his *Modern American Homes*, H. H. Von Holst captioned a photograph as illustrating "a new style of domestic architecture in and about Chicago." The photograph showed an exemplary Prairie Style house, a distinctive Midwestern residential mode that a group of Chicago architects developed at the start of the 20th century. The acknowledged leader and spokesman of the movement and the architect who produced the most noteworthy examples, including the house shown by Von Holst, was Frank Lloyd Wright (1867–1959). A number of young architects, some of whom worked in Wright's studio, also designed in the Prairie Style during its brief but prolific heyday before 1920. They included Walter Burley Griffin, Marion Mahoney, George W. Maher, William E. Drummond, William G. Purcell and George G. Elmslie, to name a few.

The architects of the Prairie School consciously rejected the academic revival styles that were popular at the time and sought to create buildings that reflected the Midwestern prairie terrain on which they were built. Wright once wrote "architecture which is really architecture proceeds from the ground." Proceeding from the ground, the Prairie house had a predominantly horizontal appearance, emphasized by a broad hipped or gabled roof and widely overhanging eaves. Often the roof was penetrated by a large, plain, rectangular chimney, the symbolic heart and hearth of the house. Prairie houses generally had two stories with walls of light-colored brick or stucco and wood. Often wings extended from the main mass at rigid right angles—there were no curves in the Prairie house. Dark wooden strips against a light stucco background revealed the influence of traditional Japanese architecture. Windows, usually casements arranged in horizontal ribbons, often featured stained glass in distinctive stylized floral or geometric patterns. One-story porches or portecochères, walls and terraces often extended from the main structure and further strengthened the horizontal appearance.

Interiors were as innovative as exteriors. The flowing interior spaces of the Queen Anne and Shingle Style served as springboards for Prairie School interiors. Space was no longer contained by four walls, at least not in major public rooms. Halls, if they could be called that anymore, flowed seamlessly into living rooms, or living areas, which in turn shared space with dining areas, which seldom had well-defined perimeters. These arrangements often made interiors seem much larger than they were, and allowed for much greater flexibility in the uses of space. Walls were plain except when accented by wooden strips, as on the exterior. Wooden trim in simple geometric shapes was used

The Robie House (1908–09, Frank Lloyd Wright), Chicago, Ill., is perhaps the most famous example of the fully developed Prairie School house. The bold interplay of horizontal planes with the solid vertical mass of the central chimney, along with the cantilevered overhangs, are identifying features of the style. (Janis J. Erins; Cervin Robinson)

for stairways, and for the built-in cabinets and furniture that architects designed to complement their houses.

The Prairie School had its greatest influence in the Chicago area, where many Prairie Style houses were built in Oak Park and other suburbs from 1900 onward. Examples can also be found throughout Illinois, Iowa and Wisconsin, as far east as Rochester, N.Y., and even on the West Coast; they generally were the work of Chicago-based architects. But the ideas of the Prairie School were also spread through publications, especially *Inland Architect*, and Prairie Style houses were designed by architects in Utah and Arizona and as far away as Puerto Rico.

After World War I, Americans embraced the comfortable associations of the revival styles so completely that the Prairie Style did not realize its full potential in the United States. The plans and philosophy of the Prairie School, however, received critical acclaim in Europe, through publication of the works of Frank Lloyd Wright. When America was again ready for cautious architectural experimentation in the 1930s, its own Prairie School movement was dead and innovative ideas had to be imported from Europe. During the

The Woodbury County Courthouse (1916–18, Purcell and Elmslie and William Steele), Sioux City, Iowa, is one of the largest Prairie Style buildings ever constructed. Its ornamentation shows some affinity to the work of Louis Sullivan. (Jack E. Boucher)

The Edward Boynton House (1907–08, Frank Lloyd Wright), Rochester, N.Y., was the eastern-most example of the Prairie Style when it was built. The chairs and tables in the dining room show that the interiors of Wright's Prairie houses were beautifully integrated with the exteriors. (Hans Padelt)

Merchants' National Bank (Poweshiek County National Bank) (1914, Louis Sullivan), Grinnell, Iowa, almost defies classification. One of a number of similar small-scale Midwestern banks, its plain brick facade with commanding cornice seems related to the Prairie Style, but the rose window in its exuberant terra-cotta surround is unique. (Robert Thall)

post–World War II construction boom of the 1950s and 1960s, Prairie Style houses reemerged in modified form with Wright's so-called Usonian Houses. Wright, who invented the name (a contraction of United States of North America), intended the type as a low-cost alternative to more conventional postwar designs. Usonian houses incorporated all the features, such as integrated spaces, of his earlier work, though they were much smaller. At about the same time, and in lesser hands than Wright's, the Prairie Style also reemerged as the ranch house, which the one-story, rigidly rectangular (with no wings), hipped-roof houses that proliferated across the country were called. This time red brick was the favored material, and the porte-cochère was rechristened the carport. Again publications, primarily magazines such as *House Beautiful, Better Homes and Gardens, Good Housekeeping* and *Sunset,* helped popularize the style.

Although the Prairie School had the largest following and the most influence in the early 20th century, other important innovations in domestic architecture were made on the West Coast. There, such pioneering architects as Bernard Maybeck, Greene and Greene and Irving Gill developed distinctive styles that survived in a limited way through the 1930s. They represent a major achievement, one of international importance, in American architectural development. However, during the first decades of the 20th century most Americans chose to live, work, shop, and pray in buildings patterned after architectural styles of the past. So far, during the first decade of the 21st century, most Americans still do.

Period Houses

Georgian Revival, Spanish Colonial Revival and even revivals of styles that had never been seen in America, as long as they had connotations of age and tradition, were popular during the first third of the 20th century, especially for residential architecture. Although the movement began before World War I, the horrors of that conflict convinced many Americans that styles reflecting their own past, with attributes of comfort, familiarity, safety and honesty were worth emulating. More modern imports from Europe were associated with Bolshevik leanings, if not worse. While each period revival house showed allegiance to one design heritage or another, the plans, site orientation and general scale of such houses were of a piece. In his *American Homes*, H. H. von Holst reproduced a series of drawings by Chicago architect Lawrence Buck that showed "the possibilities of variation on the exterior style of the house after the plan has been decided upon." Presumably the architect and client first worked out the desired plan, then determined whether they wanted "a colonial type of house with hip-roof, . . . an English type of house," or some other style.

Greystone (1925–28, Gordon B. Kaufman), Beverly Hills, Calif., incorporates details from ages past, but its overall arrangement, expansiveness and close relationship to the landscaping mark it as a period house. (Jack E. Boucher)

Styles were suggested by appropriate massing, proportions, materials and a few well-chosen details. The success of the period house depended on its stylistic accuracy. Earlier architects had, in their Queen Anne and contemporary designs, picked bits and pieces from various earlier periods. Now, architects had to become architectural historians in order to successfully suggest a specific earlier period. Most architectural offices had a library carrying the *White Pine Series*, along with books on English parish churches or farmhouses in Normandy. The *White Pine Series*, a magazine that began as a serial advertisement for white pine lumber and developed into a useful reference work, assisted in promulgating the revival of early American architecture by the Historic

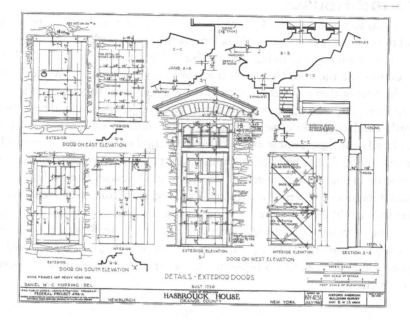

The Hasbrouck House (mid-18th century), Newburgh, N.Y., was recorded in an early HABS project. With drawings such as this, the HABS recorders in the 1930s fostered the popularity of period design. Their careful measurements made possible the authentic reproduction of features such as this doorway. (Daniel M. C. Hopping)

The Warden's House (1926), Federal Reformatory for Women, Alderson, W. Va., is based on an English precedent (seen in its half-timbering), but the plan and shape identify the structure as a period house. (Richard Cheek)

Above and below: **Caumsett Manor (1920s, John Russell Pope), Long Island, N.Y., is an exemplary country estate. Its shingle-covered barn complex and Georgian Revival garage are among the carefully designed components of the complex. (Jack E. Boucher)**

St. Matthew's Episcopal Church (1910, Willis J. Polk), San Mateo, Calif.,
a convincing period design in the Gothic mode, displays a number of
details based on English medieval prototypes. (Jack E. Boucher)

American Buildings Survey, which began its recording activities in 1933. The
first HABS drawings were produced by architects, and the fact that so many
of their sheets resemble actual working drawings reflected not only their train-
ing, but also their intention that the drawings be used in constructing new
houses based on earlier precedents.

The majority of models for period houses were farm or rural structures:
English cottages or manors, Spanish haciendas or New England farmhouses.
Most often built on large, newly plotted suburban lots and incorporating many
contemporary ideas of interior arrangement and planning, typical period
houses were far more spacious than earlier revival structures. Like Shingle
Style and Prairie School houses, period houses had an intimate relationship
with the landscape and a pronounced horizontality. Often sprawling across the
width of a lot, period houses had two yard areas, a formal front and an informal back yard. Rarely did a period house not have a rear or side terrace, porch
or patio.

The period house was not an isolated phenomenon. Many churches built at
the same time boasted details and proportions taken directly from examples
built centuries before, either in America or in Europe, while some were wholesale copies. James Gibbs's Georgian masterpiece, the church of St. Martin-in-
the-Fields in London, was a particularly favorite model. Another manifestation
of the same spirit that produced period houses and churches was the country

Stan Hywet Hall (1911–15, Charles Schneider), Akron, Ohio, is one of the grandest Tudor Revival houses in America. Built for the founder of the Goodyear Tire and Rubber Company, the mansion was modeled in part on Compton Wynates in Warwickshire, England, dating from 1480–1520. The name as well as the style harkens to the past. Stan Hywet, Anglo-Saxon for stone quarry, refers to an earlier use of the property. (Jack E. Boucher)

house. Larger than their city cousins, country houses were the centers of complexes that included stables, barns, guest houses, gardeners' cottages and similar structures. In the most developed examples, an overall architectural theme pervaded the group. The era that made these estates possible ended in the 1930s, and few of them survive in their original splendor or capacity.

The interiors of both period and country houses had fewer rooms than their 19th-century predecessors, but the rooms were much larger and space flowed more freely. Plans, however, were more formal than in bungalows, Shingle Style or Prairie Style houses. Often, especially in smaller period houses, the dining room was replaced by a dining area at one end of an oversized living room—an arrangement reflecting both the open planning and the more informal lifestyle of the times.

Although derived from historical precedent, the period house was a distinctive architectural development that was basically American. And, although the full flowering of the style occurred several decades ago, mutants of the species can be found along the curving streets of almost any suburban development.

Art Deco

By the late 1920s, new stylistic influences emanating from Europe had an impact on American architecture, which in general had been little affected by the foliated wanderings of the innovative Art Nouveau of the 1890s and early 20th century. Therefore, Art Deco, Moderne, or Modernistic, as it is variously called, was the first widely popular style in the United States to break with the revivalist tradition represented by the Beaux-Arts and period houses.

This house on Michigan Avenue, Miami Beach, Fla., displays such Art Deco elements as glass brick, horizontal bands of decoration and projecting lintel courses that afford respite from the bright Florida sun. (Walter Smalling, Jr.)

The Pan Pacific Auditorium (1935, Wurdeman and Becket), Los Angeles, Calif., has typically curved Art Deco features, such as the entrance facade marked by four pylons carefully scaled to give the building impressiveness beyond its actual size. (Marvin Rand)

Miami Beach is a treasure trove of Art Deco design. These early-20th-century hotels in the 700 block of Ocean Drive all display various aspects of the style, especially the contrast of smooth-faced walls with the details of metal, terra cotta and colored concrete.

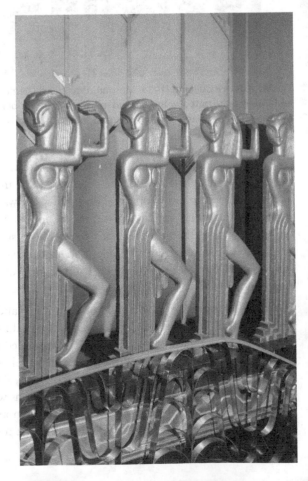

The Paramount Theater (1931, Timothy Pflueger), Oakland, Calif., is richly decorated with theatrical motifs such as these dancing ladies that grace the north wall of the grand lobby. Their stylized robes and faces harmonize with the Art Deco details surrounding them. (Jack E. Boucher)

The W. P. Story Building (1934, Morgan, Walls and Clements), Los Angeles, Calif., features bronze gates at the garage entrance that are pure examples of zigzag Moderne, with stylized floral motifs and faces. (Marvin Rand)

Art Deco takes its name from the Exposition Internationale des Arts Décoratifs et Industriels Modernes, held in Paris in 1925 as a showcase for works of "new inspiration and real originality." It was a style that consciously strove for modernity and an artistic expression to complement the machine age. Promotional literature for the "Expo Deco" stated that "reproductions, imitations and counterfeits of ancient styles will be strictly prohibited." This emphasis on the future rather than the past was one of the style's principal characteristics.

Art Deco was essentially a style of decoration and was applied to jewelry, clothing, furniture and handicrafts as well as buildings. Industrial designers created Art Deco motifs to adorn their streamlined cars, trains and kitchen appliances. Art Deco ornamentation consists largely of low-relief geometrical designs, often in the form of parallel straight lines, zigzags, chevrons and stylized floral or fountain motifs. In Europe these forms were inspired by Cubism, in America by North and South American Indian art. This ornament could be rich, varied and handcrafted or reduced to the merest suggestion for efficient machine production.

The Panhellenic Tower (1929, John Mead Howells), New York City, now the Beekman Tower, exhibits such typical Art Deco features as set-backs used as design elements and concentrations of crowning decoration. (George Eisenman)

Thomas Jefferson High School (1936, Morgan, Walls and Clements), Los Angeles, Calif., has pronounced horizontal banding, curved concave and convex surfaces and vertically articulated piers. (Marvin Rand)

Greyhound Bus Station (1938–39, George D. Brown), Columbia, S.C. This exemplary Art Moderne bus station, typical of many built throughout the country by the well-known passenger carrier, attempted to express notions of speed and modernity in its design. Glass brick, laid to form an expansive curve, aluminum, stainless steel and "Vitrolite" structural glass were among the state-of-the art, or "Moderne," materials used. (Jack E. Boucher)

Concrete, smooth-faced stone and metal were characteristic exterior architectural coverings, with accents in terra cotta, glass and colored mirrors. Polychromy, often with vivid colors, was frequently an integral part of the design. Forms were simplified and streamlined, and a futuristic effect was often sought. Although buildings clothed with Art Deco motifs exist throughout the country, the style was particularly popular in Los Angeles, Miami Beach, and New York City. Rockefeller Center (1940, Reinhard and Hofmeister; Corbett, Harrison and MacMurray; Hood, Godley and Foulihoux) is one of the most spectacular examples in New York, but the city is replete with other large office and apartment buildings with applied Art Deco ornamentation. Miami Beach even has a historic district full of first-rate examples of the style.

Merritt Parkway, South Avenue Bridge (1937, George L. Dunkelberger), New Canaan, Conn. On either side of the roadway, stepped pylons are finished with precast panels depicting stylized ornamentation reminiscent of fountains. (Jet Lowe for HAER)

Owyhee Dam (1928–32), Malheur County, Ore. When completed, this was the world's tallest dam. This detailed view of the downstream parapet wall shows the blind arcade and Art Deco light standards. (Clayton B. Fraser for HAER)

The Selig Commercial Building (1931, Arthur E. Harvey), Los Angeles, Calif., is luxuriously ornamented with black and gold terra cotta in chevron, spiral and frond designs. (Marvin Rand)

At its best, the Art Deco style produced a harmonious collaboration of effort by architects, painters, sculptors and designers. This harmony is well illustrated in some of the great movie palaces of the 1920s and 1930s, where curtains, murals and light fixtures bore the same Art Deco motifs as the buildings themselves. Art Deco was a conscious rejection of historical styles and a popular form of ornamentation. It was, however, scorned by the more intellectual practitioners of a new and even more radically iconoclastic style that began to appear in the 1930s—the International Style.

International Style

In February and March 1932, the Museum of Modern Art in New York City displayed its first architectural exhibition, entitled simply "Modern Architecture." As its catalog stated, the exhibition was intended to prove that the stylistic "confusion of the past 40 years . . . [would] shortly come to an end." Photographs and drawings of works by architects then practicing in similar styles in 15 countries were grouped under the term "International Style." In a book published by the organizers of the exhibition the same year, this new term was used as the title: *The International Style: Architecture Since 1922.* One of the organizers was Philip Johnson, who was the director of the museum's architecture department at the time. Soon he would practice what he preached, designing for himself one of the most famous modern houses of all times: the Glass House (1949) in New Canaan, Conn.

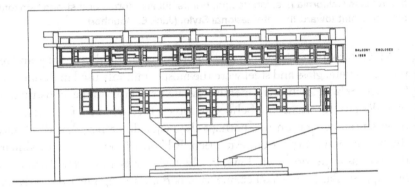

The Lovell Beach House (1926, R.M. Schindler), Newport Beach, Calif., displays remarkable force in its advancing and receding planes and its contrasts of solids and voids, yet retains a careful sense of balance. The first floor is essentially an out-door living space, protected from the elements by the second floor. (Ralston H. Nagata and Stanley A. Westfall; Marvin Rand)

The Hoover House (1919, Arthur B. Birge Clark), Stanford University, Stanford, Calif., has sculptural forms, arched openings and an intimate relation to the landscape that reflects California mission design, but its cubistic forms and strong horizontal emphasis hint toward the International Style. (Jack E. Boucher)

The International Style is based on modern structural principles and materials. Concrete, glass and steel were the most commonly used materials. While Chicago School architects merely revealed skeleton-frame construction in their designs, International School architects reveled in it. Their rejection of nonessential decoration was perhaps the major difference that distinguished the International Style from Art Deco. Ribbon windows were a hallmark of the style, as were corner windows, in which glass was mitered without any corner support. Bands of glass became as important a design feature as the bands of "curtain" that separated them. These strips of windows and solid planes helped create a horizontal feeling, another important aspect of the style, even in high-rise buildings. Here again the International Style differed from Art Deco, which frequently used setbacks, piers and other devices to create a sense of verticality. International style designers viewed a skyscraper essentially as floors of office space stacked on top of one another. In the hands of some architects and developers, such buildings could be banal; in the hands of masters, they could be eloquent. Johnson and Ludwig Mies van der Rohe produced one of the masterpieces of the style in their Seagram Building (1954–58) in New York City, with its clean, unadorned lines and rich materials.

Artificial symmetry was studiously avoided in the International Style. Balance and regularity, however, were admired and fostered. A tripartite expression of base, shaft and capital—the norm in high-rise construction of the Chicago School—was never used in the International Style. Mundane building components such as elevator shafts and compressors for air conditioning became highly visible aspects of design, and cantilevers and ground-floor piers were often used.

Many of the most famous architects who worked in 20th century America, among them Walter Gropius, Ludwig Mies van der Rohe, Richard Neutra and Marcel Breuer, started their practices in the International Style in Europe. Neutra, Viennese by birth, moved to Los Angeles in 1925, where he had a

The Farnsworth House (1949–51, Ludwig Mies van der Rohe), Plano, Ill., is a small-scale International Style design in the architect's later, more personal idiom. (Jack E. Boucher)

Fallingwater (1936, Frank Lloyd Wright), Bear Run, Pa., evokes the tenets of the International Style in its horizontal planes and dramatic cantilevers of reinforced concrete. The overall design and siting, however, mark it as an individual work of genius and one of Wright's most admired designs. (John A. Burns, AIA)

great influence. Among his major designs was the 1929 Lovell (Health) House, the first completely steel-framed house in the nation. Gropius, founder of the famous Bauhaus in his native Germany, was a team player. In 1952, after retiring from Harvard, he established The Architects Collaborative (TAC), a Cambridge, Mass., firm that received commissions across the country. In addition to Philip Johnson, American-born architects who practiced in the style included Raymond Hood and George Howe. The latter, in partnership with Swiss-born William Lescaze, designed one of the major American examples of the style—the Philadelphia Savings Fund Society (1932), known as the PSFS. Many of these architects went on to design in more personal idioms, abandoning the vigorous functionalism of the International Style. However, as a set of principles emphasizing functionalism, stark simplicity and flexible planning, the style continues to exert a great influence on modern architecture.

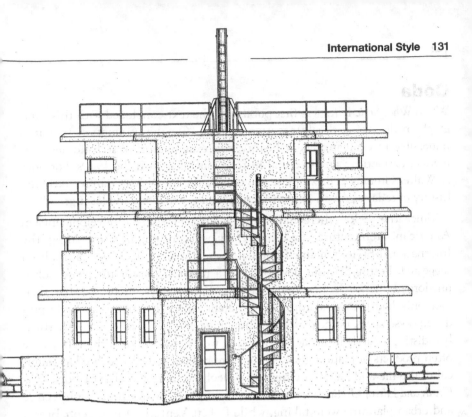

Old MARS Station (1943, Beddon, Berber, and Wharples), Fort Monroe, Va. This futuristic building served as a Military Affiliated Radio Station (MARS). Cantilevered decks, spiral stairway and ribbon windows typify the style. Built on the wall of a much earlier fort, the station is an irregularly shaped hexagon, constructed of poured concrete. (Joseph D. Balachowski, Edward F. Twohey)

Perhaps ironically, it was one of its founders—Philip Johnson—who sounded the death-knell of the International Style. As Carleton Knight cleverly phrased it in his essay on Johnson in *Master Builders* (John Wiley & Sons, 1985), "the man who introduced the glass box became the one to break it." He broke it with his design for New York City's AT&T Building (1978–84), with its famous top shaped like a broken Chippendale pediment. Widely derided at first as useless ornament, the pediment can now be seen as the harbinger of the Postmodern style. Soon many clever, and many not-so-clever, allusions to earlier architectural styles began to appear in American buildings, in a reaction to the almost too severe, too functional, too sober lines of the International Style.

Left: **Gropius House (1937, Walter Gropius with Marcel Breuer), Lincoln, Mass.** Gropius, already famous for his work at the Bauhaus, the prestigious German architectural center that he established, came to America prior to World War II to take charge of Harvard University's Graduate School of Design. His own house, with its clean, uncluttered lines, functional massing and honesty of form and materials, is one of the country's earliest expressions of the International Style. (Jack E. Boucher)

Coda

When *What Style Is It?* was first published, the text concluded with this paragraph in discussing the International Style: "On the assumption that it is impossible to evaluate recent history, this examination of stylistic developments in American architectural history concludes with the 1930s. For now, as Walter Gropius said, we must leave it "to the future historian to settle the history of today's growth in architecture, and get to work and let it grow."

Since the 1930s, there have been many new stylistic developments in American architecture, and many styles then popular, including the International Style, remained popular for many more decades. As has been suggested, Postmodernism developed as a reaction against the sleek, sober, unadorned lines of the International Style. But there was more to it than that. Not only had the standardization inherent in the International Style produced skyscrapers, office parks and shopping malls (the last two often virtually indistinguishable from each other) that were bland, if not boring, they were often products of planning ideas that were beginning to be realized as inimical to the life and fabric of cities. Jane Jacobs, in her pivotal 1961 book, *The Death and Life of Great American Cities*, challenged the directions architecture and urban planning were taking, while Robert Venturi, Denise Scott Brown and Steven Izenour, in their 1972 *Learning from Las Vegas*, argued further that the confusion and vitality of the architectural streetscape (or in the case of Las Vegas, the stripscape) should be celebrated and emulated, not denigrated and demolished. Heterogeneity, while not exactly a stylistic term per se, expresses the direction that some recent developments have taken in attempting to produce new buildings that can coexist with existing fabric. Brutalism, notably Marcel Breuer's Whitney Museum of American Art (1966) in New York City, was another reaction against the ever more sterile directions the International Style seemed to be taking. Brutalism is anything but sterile. Contextualism—where new buildings take cues and clues from their older neighbors—is perhaps the tamest approach.

Most domestic designs of recent decades, as noted in the discussion on Georgian architecture, have abandoned any attempt to reflect new technological achievements and have returned to the comfortable connotations of familiarity and past associations. In the hands of architects such as Robert A. M. Stern and Hugh Newell Jacobsen, who have taken such connotations and associations as their base, but have then built upon them in new ways, this approach has produced notable houses. Most houses now, however, are not the product of architect's designs for individual clients, but are designed and built by developers—aiming to please unknown buyers. Whether this "wave of the present" will continue as "the wave of the future" remains to be seen. When today's growth settles down, and when the extent and importance of all the recent stylistic developments can be properly assessed, the Historic American Buildings Survey will be in the forefront of recording them, just as it has been for the past 70 years.

Glossary

This glossary is a guide to common architectural terms. For more precise definitions, consult architectural dictionaries listed in the bibliography.

A

ADOBE A sun-dried, unburned brick of earth (generally clay) and straw; a structure made with such bricks.

AISLE A part of a church parallel to the nave and divided from it by piers or columns; a passageway between rows of seats, such as in a church or auditorium.

ARCADE A series of arches supported by columns or piers; a building or part of a building with a series of arches; a roofed passageway, especially one with shops on either side.

ARCHITRAVE The lower part of a classical entablature, resting directly on the capital of a column; the molding around a window or door.

ASHLAR Hewn or squared stone, also masonry of such stone; a thin, dressed rectangle of stone for facing walls, also called ashlar veneer.

ASTYLAR Without columns or pilasters.

AXIALITY Symmetrical disposition of parts of a building or of structures along an axis.

B

BALUSTER An upright, often vase-shaped, support for a rail.

BALUSTRADE A series of balusters with a rail.

BAND WINDOWS A horizontal series of uniform windows that appear to have little or no separation between them.

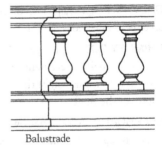
Balustrade

BAPTISTERY A part of a church; formerly, a separate building used for baptism.

BARGEBOARD A board, often ornately carved, attached to the projecting edges of a gabled roof; sometimes referred to as verge-board.

BATTER The receding upward slope of a wall or structure.

BATTLEMENT A parapet built with indentations for defense or decoration.

BAY One unit of a building that consists of a series of similar units, commonly defined by the number of window and door openings per floor or by the space between columns or piers.

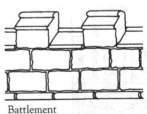
Battlement

BELT COURSE A narrow horizontal band projecting from the exterior walls of a building, usually defining the interior floor levels.

BLIND ARCH An arch that does not contain an opening for a window or door but is set against or indented within a wall.

BRACE A diagonal stabilizing member of a building frame.

BRACKET A support element under eaves, shelves or other overhangs, often more decorative than functional.

BUTTRESS A projecting structure of masonry or wood for supporting or giving stability to a wall or building.

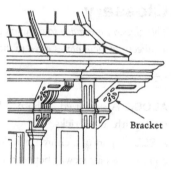

Bracket

C

CANTILEVER A projecting beam or part of a structure supported only at one end.

CAPITAL The top, decorated part of a column or pilaster crowning the shaft and supporting the entablature.

CARTOUCHE An ornamental panel in the form of a scroll, circle or oval, often bearing an inscription.

CASEMENT A window with sash hung vertically and opening inward or outward.

CASTELLATED Having battlements and turrets, like a medieval castle.

CAST IRON Iron, shaped in a mold, that is brittle, hard and cannot be welded; in 19th-century American commercial architecture, cast-iron units were used frequently to form entire facades.

CHEVRON A V-shaped decoration generally used as a continuous molding.

CHIMNEY POT A pipe placed on top of a chimney, usually of earthenware, that functions as a continuation of the flue and improves the draft.

Chevron

CLAPBOARD A long, narrow board with one edge thicker than the other, overlapped to cover the outer walls of frame structures; also known as weatherboard.

CLASSICAL Pertaining to the architecture of ancient Greece and Rome.

CLERESTORY The upper part of the nave, transepts and choir of a church containing windows; also, any similar windowed wall or construction used for light and ventilation.

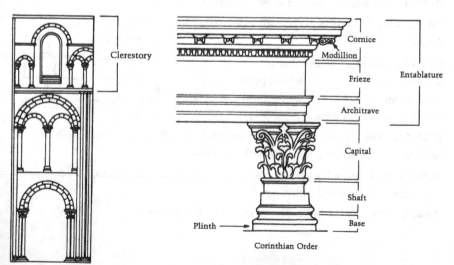

Clerestory

Cornice
Modillion
Frieze
Entablature
Architrave
Capital
Shaft
Plinth
Base

Corinthian Order

CORBEL A bracket or block projecting from the face of a wall that generally supports a cornice, beam or arch.

CORINTHIAN ORDER The most ornate of the classical Greek orders of architecture, characterized by a slender fluted column with a bell-shaped capital decorated with stylized acanthus leaves; variations of this order were extensively used by the Romans.

CORNICE In classical architecture, the upper, projecting section of an entablature; projecting ornamental molding along the top of a building or wall.

COURSED MASONRY A wall with continuous horizontal layers of stone or brick.

CRENELLATION A battlement.

CROCKET In Gothic architecture, carved projections in the shape of stylized leaves that decorate the edges of spires, gables and pinnacles.

CUPOLA A dome-shaped roof on a circular base, often set on the ridge of a roof.

Crocket

DEPENDENCY A structure subordinate to or serving as an adjunct to a main building.

DORIC ORDER The oldest and simplest of the classical Greek orders, characterized by heavy fluted columns with no base, plain saucer-shaped capitals and a bold simple cornice.

DORMER A vertically set window on a sloping roof; the roofed structure housing such a window.

DOUBLE-HUNG SASH WINDOW A window with two sashes, one above the other, arranged to slide vertically past each other.

DOUBLE PORTICO A projecting two-story porch with columns and a pediment.

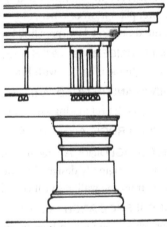

Doric Order

EAVES The projecting overhang at the lower edge of a roof.

EGG-AND-DART MOLDING A decorative molding comprising alternating egg-shaped and dart-shaped motifs.

ENTABLATURE In classical architecture, the part of a structure between the column capital and the roof or pediment, comprising the architrave, frieze and cornice.

EYEBROW DORMER A low dormer in which the arched roofline forms a reverse curve at each end, giving it the general outline of an eyebrow.

FANLIGHT A semicircular or fan-shaped window with radiating members or tracery set over a door or window.

FENESTRATION The arrangement of windows in a wall.

FESTOON A carved, molded or painted garland of fruit, flowers or leaves suspended between two points in a curve.

FINIAL An ornament at the top of a spire, gable or pinnacle.

FLEMISH GABLE A gable with stepped and occasionally multicurved sides, derived from 16th-century, Dutch prototypes.

FLUTED Having regularly spaced vertical, parallel grooves or "flutes," as on the shaft of a column, pilaster or other surface.

FOLIATED Decorated with leaf ornamentation or a design comprising arcs or lobes.

G

GABLE A triangular wall segment at the end of a double-pitched or gabled roof.

GALLERY A roofed promenade, colonnade or corridor; an outdoor balcony; in the South, a porch or veranda.

GAMBREL A ridged roof with two slopes on each side, the lower slope having the steeper pitch.

Gambrel

H

HACIENDA In Spanish-speaking countries or areas influenced by Spain, a large estate, plantation or ranch; also, the house of the ranch owner; in the southwestern United States, a low sprawling house with projecting roof and wide porches.

HALF-TIMBERING Wall construction in which the spaces between members of the timber frame are filled with brick, stone or other material.

HEWN AND PEGGED A frame construction system in which the beams are hewn with an adze (predating saws) and joined by large wooden pegs.

HIPPED ROOF A roof with four uniformly pitched sides.

HOOD MOLDING A large molding over a window, originally designed to direct water away from the wall; also called a drip molding.

HORSESHOE ARCH An arch shaped like a horseshoe; common in Islamic architecture.

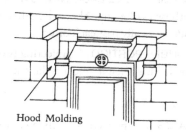

Hood Molding

Ionic Order

IONIC ORDER An order of classical Greek architecture characterized by a capital with two opposed volutes.

L

LANCET A narrow pointed arch.

LANTERN A structure built on the top of a roof with open or windowed walls.

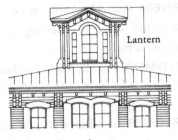

Lantern

LEADED GLASS Small panes of glass held in place with lead strips; the glass may be clear or stained.

LEAN-TO A simple structural addition that has a single-pitch roof.

LOZENGE A diamond-shaped decorative motif.

M

MANSARD ROOF A roof that has two slopes on all four sides.

MASONRY Wall construction of materials such as stone, brick and adobe.

MEASURED DRAWING An exact-scale drawing based on measurements taken from an existing building.

MEDALLION An object resembling a large medal or coin.

MINARET A tall, slender tower attached to a mosque with one or more projecting balconies.

MITER The edge of a piece of material, generally wood, that has been beveled preparatory to making a joint.

MODILLION An ornamental bracket or console used in series under the cornice of the Corinthian order and others.

MOLDED BRICK Brick shaped in a mold, commonly in decorative shapes.

MOLDING A continuous decorative band that is either carved into or applied to a surface.

MULLION A vertical member separating (and often supporting) windows, doors or panels set in a series.

N

NAVE The long, narrow main part of a church that rises higher than the flanking aisles.

NOGGING The brick or rubble material used to fill the spaces between wooden frames.

O

OBELISK A tall, four-sided shaft that is tapered and crowned with a pyramidal point.

ORDER Any of several specific styles of classical and Renaissance architecture characterized by the type of column used (e.g., Doric, Ionic, Corinthian, Composite, Tuscan).

P

PALLADIAN WINDOW A tripartite window opening with a large arched central light and flanking rectangular side lights.

PARAPET A low, solid, protective wall or railing along the edge of a roof or balcony.

PATERA A circular ornament used in decorative relief work.

PAVILION A part of a building projecting from the rest; an ornamental structure in a garden or park.

PEDIMENT A wide, low-pitched gable surmounting the facade of a building in a classical style; any similar triangular crowning element used over doors, windows and niches.

PILASTER A shallow pier attached to a wall; often decorated to resemble a classical column.

PLINTH The base of a pedestal, column or statue; a continuous course of stones supporting a wall.

PODIUM A low platform or base.

POLYCHROMY The use of many colors in decoration, especially in architecture and statuary.

PORTAL The principal entry of a structure or wall of a city.

PORTE-COCHÈRE A large covered entrance porch through which vehicles can be driven.

PORTICO A major porch, usually with a pedimented roof supported by classical columns.

PRESSED METAL Thin sheets of metal molded into decorative designs and used to cover interior walls and ceilings.

PUEBLO An Indian community in the Southwest with distinctive flat-roofed structures of adobe and stone.

Q

QUOIN Units of stone or brick used to accentuate the corners of a building.

Quoin

R

REEDED Decoration of parallel convex moldings (the opposite of fluted).

REREDOS An ornamental screen behind an altar.

REVEAL The vertical side of a door or window opening between the frame and the wall surface.

RINCEAU A band of ornament consisting of intertwining foliage.

ROCOCO The decorative style developed from the baroque; characterized by delicacy, light colors and a general reduction in building scale.

ROSETTE Stylized floral decoration.

RUSTICATION Masonry cut in massive blocks separated from each other by deep joints.

Reveal

S

SALTBOX A gabled-roof house in which the rear slope is much longer than the front.

SASH A frame in which the panes of a window are set.

SETBACK An architectural expedient in which the upper stories of a tall building are stepped back from the lower stories; designed to permit more light to reach street level.

SHAFT The main part of a column between the base and capital.

SKELETON FRAME A freestanding frame of iron or steel that supports the weight of a building and on which the floors and outer covering are hung.

SPANDREL The triangular space between adjacent arches and the horizontal molding, cornice or framework above them; in skeleton frame construction, the horizontal panels below and above windows between the continuous vertical piers.

SPINDLE A turned wooden element, often used in screens, stair railings and porch trim.

STAIR HALL A room specifically designed to contain a staircase.

STAIR TOWER A projecting tower that contains a staircase serving all floors; usually found in castles and châteaux.

STRINGCOURSE A narrow, continuous ornamental band set in the face of a building as a design element; also known as a cordon.

SWAG A festoon in which the object suspended resembles a piece of draped cloth.

T

TERRA COTTA A fine-grained, brown-red, fired clay used for roof tiles and decoration; literally, cooked earth.

TRACERY The curved mullions of a stone-framed window; ornamental work of pierced patterns in or on a screen, window glass or panel.

TREFOIL A design of three lobes, similar to a cloverleaf.

TUDOR ARCH A low, wide, pointed arch common in the architecture of Tudor England.

TURRET A small, slender tower usually at the corner of a building, often containing a circular stair.

V

VAULT An arched ceiling of masonry.

VERANDA A roofed open gallery or porch.

VIGA A wooden beam used in a series to support the roof of an Indian pueblo structure; the ends usually project through the outer walls.

VOLUTE A spiral, scroll-like ornament.

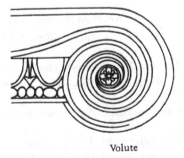

Volute

W

WATTLE AND DAUB A method of construction with thin branches (wattles) plastered over with clay mud (daub).

WEATHERBOARD Clapboard; wooden siding.

Further Reading

This reading list includes books dealing with the development of American architecture. Most are of a general nature, but some discuss specific styles. Several architectural dictionaries are included for further explanation of terms in the glossary and more specific terms that are not included.

Andrews, Wayne. *Architecture, Ambition and Americans*. New York: Free Press, 1964.

————. *Architecture in America: A Photographic History from the Colonial Period to the Present*. 1960. Rev. ed. New York: Atheneum, 1977.

Blumenson, John J. G. *Identifying American Architecture: A Pictorial Guide to Styles and Terms, 1600–1945*. Nashville: American Association for State and Local History, 1977. Rev. ed. New York: Norton, 1981.

Brooks, H. Allen. *The Prairie School: Frank Lloyd Wright and His Midwest Contemporaries*. Toronto: University of Toronto Press, 1972.

Burchard, John, and Bush-Brown, Albert. *The Architecture of America: A Social and Cultural History*. Boston: Little, Brown, 1961.

Carrott, Richard G. *The Egyptian Revival: Its Sources, Monuments and Meaning, 1808–1858*. Berkeley: University of California Press, 1978.

Condit, Carl W. *American Building: Materials and Techniques from the First Colonial Settlements to the Present*. Chicago: University of Chicago Press, 1969.

————. *The Chicago School of Architecture*. Chicago: University of Chicago Press, 1964.

Downing, Andrew Jackson. *The Architecture of Country Houses*. 1850. Reprint. New York: Dover, 1969.

Drexler, Arthur. *The Architecture of the École des Beaux-Arts*. New York: Museum of Modern Art, 1977.

Fitch, James Marston. *American Building: The Historical Forces that Shaped It*. Boston: Houghton Mifflin, 1966.

————. *American Building 2: The Environmental Forces that Shaped It*. Boston: Houghton Mifflin, 1972.

Fleming, John; Honour, Hugh; and Pevsner, Nikolaus. *The Penguin Dictionary of Architecture*. 1966. Rev. ed. Baltimore: Penguin Books, 1983.

Ghirado, Diane. *Architecture after Modernism*. London: Thames and Hudson, 1996.

Giedion, Siegfried. *Space, Time and Architecture: The Growth of a New Tradition*. 1941. 5th ed. Cambridge: Harvard University Press, 1972.

Girouard, Mark. *Sweetness and Light: The Queen Anne Movement, 1860–1900*. New York: Oxford University Press, 1977.

Gowans, Alan. *The Comfortable House: North American Suburban Architecture,* *1890–1930.* Cambridge: MIT Press, 1986.

_____. *Images of American Living: Four Centuries of Architecture and Furniture as* *Cultural Expression.* 1964. Reprint. New York: Harper and Row, 1976.

Hamlin, Talbot. *Greek Revival Architecture in America.* 1944. Reprint. New York: Harper and Row, 1976.

Hammett, Ralph W. *Architecture in the United States: A Survey of Architectural Styles* *Since 1776.* New York: John Wiley & Sons, 1976.

Harris, Cyril M. *Dictionary of Architecture and Construction.* New York: McGraw-Hill, 1975.

Hitchcock, Henry-Russell. *The Architecture of H. H. Richardson and His Times.* 1936. 2nd ed., rev. Cambridge: MIT Press, 1966.

_____. *Architecture: Nineteenth and Twentieth Centuries.* 1958. 1963. 2nd ed. Reprint. Baltimore: Penguin Books, 1971.

_____. *In the Nature of Materials: The Buildings of Frank Lloyd Wright, 1887–1941.* 1942. Reprint. New York: Da Capo, 1973.

Hitchcock, Henry-Russell, and Johnson, Philip. *The International Style: Architecture* *Since 1922.* 1932. Reprint. New York: Norton, 1966.

Hunt, William Dudley, Jr. *Encyclopedia of American Architecture.* New York: McGraw-Hill, 1980.

Jordy, William H. *American Buildings and Their Architects. Vol. III: Progressive and* *Academic Ideals at the Turn of the Twentieth Century.* Garden City, N.Y.: Doubleday, 1972.

_____. *American Buildings and Their Architects. Vol. IV: The Impact of European* *Modernism in the Mid-Twentieth Century.* Garden City, N.Y.: Doubleday, 1972.

Kennedy, Roger. *Greek Revival America.* New York: Steward, Tabori and Chang, 1989.

Kidney, Walter C. *The Architecture of Choice: Eclecticism in America, 1880–1930.* New York: Braziller, 1974.

Kimball, Fiske. *Thomas Jefferson, Architect.* 1916. Reprint. New York: Da Capo Press, 1968.

Lancaster, Clay. *The American Bungalow, 1880–1920's.* New York: Abbeville, 1984.

Loth, Calder, and Sadler, Julius Trousdale, Jr. *The Only Proper Style.* Boston: New York Graphic Society, 1976.

Lee, Antoinette J. *Architects to the Nation: The Rise and Decline of the Supervising* *Architect's Office.* New York: Oxford University Press, 2000.

Maddex, Diane, ed. *Master Builders: A Guide to Famous American Architects*. Washington, D.C.: The Preservation Press, 1985.

McAlester, Virginia and Lee. *A Field Guide to American Houses*. New York: Knopf, 1984.

McClelland, Linda Flint. *Presenting Nature: The Historic Landscape Design of the National Park Service, 1916 to 1942*. Washington, D.C.: U.S. Government Printing Office, 1993.

McCoy, Esther. *Five California Architects*. New York: Reinhold, 1960.

Maass, John. *The Gingerbread Age: A View of Victorian America*. 1957. Reprint. New York: Greenwich House, Crown, 1983.

_____. *The Victorian Home in America*. New York: Hawthorn Books, 1972.

Morrison, Hugh. *Early American Architecture: From the First Colonial Settlements to the National Period*. New York: Oxford University Press, 1952.

Mumford, Lewis. *The Brown Decades: A Study of the Arts in America, 1865–1895*. 1931. Reprint. New York: Dover, 1955.

_____. *Sticks and Stones: A Study of American Architecture and Civilization*. 1924. Reprint. New York: Dover, 1955.

Mumford, Lewis (ed.). *Roots of Contemporary American Architecture: 37 Essays from the Mid-nineteenth Century to the Present*. 1952. Reprint. New York: Dover, 1972.

National Trust for Historic Preservation; Wrenn, Tony P.; and Mulloy, Elizabeth. *America's Forgotten Architecture*. New York: Pantheon Books, 1976.

Naylor, Gillian. *The Arts and Crafts Movement: A Study of Its Sources, Ideals and Influence on Design Theory*. Cambridge: MIT Press, 1971.

Newcomb, Rexford. *Spanish Colonial Architecture in the United States*. Locust Valley, N.Y.: J. J. Augustin, 1938.

Peterson, Charles E. (ed.). *Building Early America*. Philadelphia: Chilton, 1976.

Pierson, William H., Jr. *American Buildings and Their Architects, Vol. 1: The Colonial and Neoclassical Styles*. Garden City, N.Y.: Doubleday, 1970.

_____. *American Buildings and Their Architects: Technology and the Picturesque; The Corporate and the Early Gothic Styles*. Garden City, N.Y.: Doubleday, 1978.

Placzek, Adolf K. (ed.). *The Macmillan Encyclopedia of Architects*. New York: Macmillan, 1982.

Rifkind, Carole. *A Field Guide to American Architecture*. New York: New American Library, 1980

Robinson, Cervin and Bletter, Rosemary Haag. *Skyscraper Style: Art Deco New York*. New York: Oxford University Press, 1975.

Roth, Leland M. *A Concise History of American Architecture*. New York: Harper and Row, 1979.

Saylor, Henry H. *Dictionary of Architecture*. 1952. Reprint. New York: John Wiley & Sons, 1963.

Scully, Vincent J., Jr. *The Shingle Style and the Stick Style: Architectural Theory and Design from Richardson to the Origins of Wright*. 1955. Rev. ed. New Haven, Conn.: Yale University Press, 1971.

Schweitser, Robert, and Davis, Michael W. R. *America's Favorite Homes: Mail-Order Catalogues as a Guide to Popular Early 20th Century Houses*. Detroit: Wayne State University Press, 1990.

Smith, G. E. Kidder. *Architecture in America: A Pictorial History*. New York: American Heritage, 1976.

Stamm, Alicia, and Peatross, C. Ford, eds. *Historic America: Buildings, Structures, and Sites*. Historic American Buildings Survey/Historic American Engineering Record. Washington, D.C.: Library of Congress, 1983.

Stanton, Phoebe B. *The Gothic Revival and American Church Architecture: An Episode in Taste, 1840–1856*. Baltimore: Johns Hopkins University Press, 1968.

Stevenson, Katherine Cole, and Jandl, H. Ward. *Houses by Mail: A Guide to Houses from Sears, Roebuck and Company*. Washington, D.C.: The Preservation Press, 1986.

Walker, Lester. *American Shelter: An Illustrated Encyclopedia of the American Home*. New York: Overlook Press, Viking, 1981.

Waterman, Thomas T. *Domestic Colonial Architecture of Tidewater, Virginia*. 1932. Reprint. New York: Da Capo Press, 1968.

Whiffen, Marcus. *American Architecture Since 1780: A Guide to the Styles*. Cambridge: MIT Press, 1969.

Whiffen, Marcus, and Koeper, Frederick. *American Architecture, 1607–1976*. Cambridge: MIT Press, 1981.

Wilson, Richard, Pilgrim, Dianne, and Murray, Richard N. *The American Renaissance: 1876–1917*. New York: Pantheon, 1979.

Winter, Robert. *The California Bungalow*. Los Angeles: Hennessey and Ingalls, 1980.

Information Sources

The following organizations and agencies can provide further information on architects, American architecture and the preservation of historic buildings. For archive and photograph collections on specific architects, consult the resources listed in Further Reading.

American Institute of Architects (AIA)
1735 New York Avenue, N.W.
Washington, D.C. 20006
http://www.aia.org
(800) AIA-3837

American Society of Civil Engineers (ASCE)
1801 Alexander Bell Drive
Reston, VA 20191-4400
http://www.asce.org
(800) 548-2723

American Society of Landscape Architects (ASLA)
636 Eye Street, N.W.
Washington, D.C. 20001-3736
http://www.asla.org
(888) 999-2752

Historic American Buildings Survey & Historic American Engineering Record (HABS/HAER)
National Park Service
U.S. Department of the Interior
1849 C Street, N.W. (2270)
Washington, D.C. 20005
http://www.cr.nps.gov/habshaer/
(202) 354-2135

Center for American Architecture, Design and Engineering Project
Library of Congress
Prints and Photographs Division
Washington, D.C. 20540-4730
http://www.loc.gov/rr/print/
(202) 707-8695

National Building Museum (NBM)
401 F Street, N.W.
Washington, D.C. 20001
http://www.nbm.org
(202) 272-2448

National Register of Historic Places
National Park Service
U.S. Department of the Interior
1201 Eye Street (MS 2280)
Washington, D.C. 20005
http://www.cr.nps.gov/nr
(202) 354-2213

National Trust for Historic Preservation
1785 Massachusetts Avenue, N.W.
Washington, D.C. 20036
http://www.nationaltrust.org
(800) 944-6847

Regional Offices

Northeast Regional Office
Seven Faneuil Hall Marketplace
Boston, MA 02109
(617) 523-0885

Mid-Atlantic Regional Office
6401 Germantown Avenue
Philadelphia, PA 19144
(215) 848-8033

Southern Regional Office
456 King Street
Charleston, SC 29403
(843) 722-8552

Midwest Regional Office
53 West Jackson Boulevard
Suite 350
Chicago, IL 60604
(312) 939-5547

Mountains/Plains Regional Office
511 16th Street
Suite 700
Denver, CO 80202
(303) 623-1504

Southwest Regional Office
500 Main Street
Suite 1030
Fort Worth, TX 76102
(817) 332-4398

Western Regional Office
8 California Street
Suite 400
San Francisco, CA 94111-4828
(415) 956-0610

Southern California Regional Office
1821 Hanscom Drive
South Pasadena, CA 91030
(323) 341-7031

Society of Architectural Historians (SAH)
1365 North Astor Street
Chicago, IL 60610-2144
http://www.sah.com
(312) 573-1365

About HABS/HAER

The Historic American Buildings Survey (HABS) and its sister programs, the Historic American Engineering Record (HAER) and the Historic American Landscapes Survey (HALS), are integral parts of the National Park Service's historic preservation programs. Established on a permanent basis in 1934 through a tripartite agreement between the service, the Library of Congress and the American Institute of Architects, HABS records significant buildings and sites in the United States and its territories through measured architectural drawings, large-format photographs, and written histories. The Library of Congress preserves the documentation for HABS and makes the material available to the public in both analog and digital formats in the library's Prints & Photographs Division Reading Room in Washington, D.C., and through its "Built in America" web site:

http://memory.loc.gov/ammem/hhhtml/hhhome.html

The HABS collection consists of documentation on more than 30,000 historic structures throughout the United States and its territories. The documentation contains over 51,000 sheets of measured drawings, more than 156,000 large-format black-and-white photographs, and more than 30,000 original historical reports. Reports on deposit at the Library of Congress are arranged geographically: first by state, then by county and city (or vicinity). Approximately 20,000 reproductions of individual items in the collection are made each year for architects, historic preservationists, scholars and the general public, making it one of the most utilized collections at the Library of Congress.

Most of the items in the HABS collection are now available in digital format and may be viewed and downloaded at no cost from the Library of Congress's Built in America web site (see above). Currently, visitors to the site may search the collection database by keyword, subject or geographic location. A multiyear cataloging effort is in progress, which, once complete, will facilitate searches by building type, significant features, industrial and cultural context, media, genre and other categories.

The Library of Congress maintains a list of publications on various state and local surveys conducted by HABS and its sister programs, including all published catalogs, as well as a list of publications that reproduce substantial portions of the collections. Researchers may request an information packet from the Prints & Photographs Division providing reading and price lists and basic information on the HABS and other collections.

Copies of HABS material at the Library of Congress may be ordered from the library's photoduplication service via mail or fax. Details on how to place an order may be obtained online at http://lcweb.loc.gov/preserv/pds/habshaer.html or by contacting the photoduplication service via telephone at (202) 707-5640, via fax at (202) 707-1771, or via e-mail at photoduplication@loc.gov. In most cases, the photographs and measured drawings published in this book, as well as supplemental historical information on the buildings pictured, may be ordered in this manner or downloaded from the Built in America site. Materials from recent projects may not be immediately available for reproduction.

Index